In the Company
of Prophets

In the Company of Prophets

Personal Experiences
of D. Arthur Haycock with
Heber J. Grant, George Albert Smith,
David O. McKay, Joseph Fielding Smith,
Harold B. Lee, Spencer W. Kimball,
and Ezra Taft Benson

By Heidi S. Swinton

Deseret Book Company
Salt Lake City, Utah

Photo Credits:

Front cover and pages 94, 105, and 117 courtesy of *Deseret News:* front cover by Tom Smart, pages 94 and 117 by Gerald W. Silver, and page 105 by Gerry Avant. Used by permission.

Pages 11 and 63 courtesy *Salt Lake Tribune.* Used by permission.

Pages 13, 36, 64, 71, 74, and back cover courtesy LDS Church: page 71 and back cover by Jed A. Clark. Used by permission.

Pages 17, 19, 26, 40, 46, 49, 60, and 89 courtesy D. Arthur Haycock. Used by permission.

Page 52 is a *Honolulu Star-Bulletin* photo.

Page 115 is a U.S. Department of Agriculture photo by Forsythe.

Library of Congress Cataloging-in-Publication Data.

Swinton, Heidi S., 1948–
    In the company of prophets / by Heidi S. Swinton.
        p. cm.
    Includes index.
    ISBN 0-87579-704-0
    1. Haycock, D. Arthur (David Arthur), 1916–   . 2. Church of Jesus Christ of Latter-day Saints—Employees—Biography. 3. Private secretaries—United States—Biography. 4. Mormon Church—Employees—Biography. 5. Church of Jesus Christ of Latter-day Saints—Presidents—Biography. I. Title.
II. Title.
BX8695.H39A3   1993
289.3'092—dc20

                                                    [B] 93-12875
                                                          CIP

Printed in the United States of America

10   9   8   7   6   5   4   3   2   1

Contents

Introduction

For more than half of the twentieth century, David Arthur Haycock has enjoyed a personal, intense, panoramic view of Church leadership. Closely associated with seven presidents of the Church in this dispensation, he has spent more waking time with the prophets of the Lord than have their families or other General Authorities.

Having worked with Church Presidents Heber J. Grant, George Albert Smith, David O. McKay, Joseph Fielding Smith, Harold B. Lee, Spencer W. Kimball, and Ezra Taft Benson, he affirms, "Each has had his own inspiration and his own mission. Each was raised up by the Lord for a special time and need. The Lord listens to them, and they listen to the Lord."

His experiences were one of a kind. In 1935, as a young missionary in Hawaii, he raised his hand with hundreds of other island Saints when President Heber J. Grant organized the first stake outside the continental United States. He sat at the bedside of President George Albert Smith and held his hand as he died. While serving as a mission president in Hawaii, he toured the islands with President David O. McKay. He worked for President Ezra Taft Benson when he served as Secretary of Agriculture in Washington, D.C. He accompanied President Joseph Fielding Smith to England for the first LDS area conference in 1971. He was alone with President Harold B. Lee when he died. He transcribed from

President Spencer W. Kimball's dictation the declaration giving the priesthood to all worthy males of The Church of Jesus Christ of Latter-day Saints.

"I've had more tutoring and training from the real masters of life than anybody who ever went to college," Arthur is quick to say. For these singular servants, he has kept their journals, recorded their speeches, packed their suitcases, read their conference addresses when they were too ill to speak, and sometimes even shined their shoes. For more than fifty years, his life has been a unique odyssey in the company of prophets.

For Arthur, the experience has never been common: "I never took it for granted. Anybody else would have done the same things, and they, too, would have counted it a privilege. I am grateful for the opportunity to have been close by. I have shared their experiences all over the world, their joys and their disappointments. They lost loved ones. They were human, and I guess that is the greatest thing about it. They were real."

Arthur took his work seriously, though he quietly stayed in the background. He explains, "If you don't have the Brethren's total confidence, if they can't talk about anything or anyone, any situation or circumstance with you sitting there, it doesn't work." But his fervor and discretion in the position were always evident. Here was a man who loved his work and loved his boss.

His interests were never selfish. "What made the president happy made me happy," he says, "and anything that troubled him troubled me. I didn't have the responsibility or the stewardship that he carried, of course, but I felt responsible to help him do his work, any time of the day or night."

That was not idle commitment, for Arthur's job was more than full time. Serving these men and assisting them in their work was not just a job; it was his life. Though the job description changed with each president, Arthur's dedication to each prophet never wavered. In addition to keeping minutes, writing letters, scheduling, telephoning, organizing, filing, reviewing data, and writing and redirecting inquiries, he was also chauffeur, tour guide, valet, chef, doctor, friend, confidant, and security guard. He went on diets with President Spencer W. Kimball and ate boiled wheat with President George Albert Smith. He delivered Christmas gifts for President Harold B. Lee and bought watermelon, even out of season, for President Joseph Fielding Smith. Arthur was not involved in making a name for himself or in formulating policies for the Church. His assignment, as with other Latter-day Saints, was to serve the Lord every day, applying gospel teachings to daily experiences. That his service was to the president of the Church made the circumstances unique, but the principles were the same.

Each president had his own ways of operating that adapted to changes in the size and complexity of the growing international church. When assisting President George Albert Smith, Arthur would often accompany the president home for lunch, Arthur driving the president's car.

There was a time when crowds would gather outside the back door of the Tabernacle to chat with the president after general conference. Though security became an issue in the 1970s, President Kimball still charged into the crowd to shake hands at every opportunity because he loved being with the people so much.

Over the years, the pictures of Arthur standing beside each president show a gradual change—his hair turns from black to steel gray to snow white—but his countenance has never altered. He has stood stalwart and supportive of the prophets, committed to their singular mission and methods. Arthur is not weary from a life of church service. In the process of his daily work, he has seen and heard much and gained confidence in the total gospel plan. He is matter-of-fact, realistic, and fiercely loyal.

For more than fifty years, Arthur has had his eye on the progress of the Church. Certainly a life spent with latter-day prophets intrigues most members and observers who would like just a glimpse of what Arthur has seen. But his memories are not sensational. He didn't keep a journal or even notes on a calendar of his own. He does not describe himself as a major player. He has focused on facilitating the work of the president of The Church of Jesus Christ of Latter-day Saints. His loyalty and purpose is clear in each expression of love for these prophets and admiration for all they accomplished.

When Arthur sat down at his desk in the Church Administration Building on September 8, 1938, he had no idea what was ahead. For him, just getting a job at the Church had been a six-month crusade, and he was delighted to be one of a handful of full-time employees.

It would be another five years before Spencer W. Kimball or Ezra Taft Benson would be called to serve as apostles in the Council of the Twelve. President Grant presided over the largely North American church with its 750,000 members, eighteen missions, and 124 stakes. The Church office staff worked six days a week (until 1:00 P.M. on Saturday) and was spread out on all five floors of the granite administration building at 47 East South Temple Street.

Arthur's office in the Finance Department was located on the main level in a large room with bare floors, a rubber mat under each chair, and a central telephone on the counter. The staff took turns taking the calls. The Church offices had three phone lines and a small PBX board for outside calls and for the use of the Brethren. Three people ran the Missionary Department.

General conference was not yet broadcast on radio, though microphones had recently been installed in the Tabernacle. Television, still in its infancy, was not used for public broadcast of conference sessions until 1949. Instead of using the now-familiar red armchairs on the stand, the General Authorities, totaling twenty-six, sat on padded red benches. Every one of the authorities spoke at conference, and the meetings, with no broadcasting time constraints, lasted as long as the speakers chose to speak. "They could just get up and preach to the people as long as they felt prompted," says Arthur.

Years later, the sessions were timed down to the minute, including choir numbers or organ interludes to fill in if someone sat down too soon. When Arthur retired as secretary to President Ezra Taft Benson to preside over the Hawaii Temple in 1986, his third mission to the Islands, the Church offices had more than filled the twenty-eight-floor high-rise office building completed in 1972 at 50 East North Temple. Times had changed.

Arthur's first responsibility was preparing the paychecks on a manual Underwood typewriter for all Church employees. He also dispensed funds to missionaries all over the world. Parents brought or sent in money, which Arthur converted to marks, francs, guilders, or pounds sterling and then dispersed through the Church's International Exchange Agency to mission presidents.

At twenty-two he was one of the youngest Church employees. Hired by Arthur Winter, who had been hired by Brigham Young, Arthur Haycock was referred to as "the boy" by fellow employees Carl Carlson and Cannon Lund. In some ways the reference stuck. Thirty years later when he drove President Joseph Fielding Smith home after a full day at the office, the prophet remarked to his daughter, "He's a good boy."

Age was something Arthur came to understand well in his years at the Church. He learned firsthand, again and again, that the Lord has a timetable. He says, "I have watched great men be trained, mellowed, and molded by the Lord. Then I've watched them grow old, struggle, and die. It's a hard period when their health fails, and yet the Lord is always in charge and always with us. Each was prepared for a particular time, need, and circumstance. That's the way the Lord ordained it."

Arthur saw six presidents of the Twelve called to preside over the Church. "Given the pattern, the president will probably always be an older man," he says. "They have years of training, often several decades, and a vast treasure of experiences before they are called to act as the Lord's chosen mouthpiece and preside over the whole Church."

Indeed, they have responsibility for all people. The magnitude of such a calling is unique to The Church of Jesus Christ of Latter-day Saints. And it should be, says Arthur: "These brethren are citizens of the world. They become that as the Church grows. They know the people, and the people know them and love them—they support and pray for them. Whether it is in a little hogan, an adobe hut, a new home in the suburbs, or a modest flat in a large city, it doesn't matter. The prayers and support of the members sustain these men who carry such a burden and responsibility."

But such devotion takes its toll. "They are out in front all of the time, and they get tired and worn," says Arthur. "I've seen many of the Brethren come and go, men whom I love and respect and admire and whom the Lord has called and sustained as prophets, seers, and revelators. To see them become weak and tired, unable to do things; to see great men, stalwart and dynamic, grow old is a challenge for us all. I have seen the pattern repeated time and again with Presidents Heber J. Grant, George Albert Smith, David O. McKay, Joseph Fielding Smith, Harold B. Lee, Spencer W. Kimball, and Ezra Taft Benson."

Of them all, only President Lee was taken while still in the height of his vigor. Presidents Joseph Fielding Smith, David O. McKay, and Spencer W. Kimball because of poor health played less visible roles in their later years as president. Arthur says: "I raced to President Joseph Fielding Smith's side, arriving at the home of his daughter Amelia and son-in-law Bruce R. McConkie shortly after the president died. I joined President Lee at the McKay apartment in the Hotel Utah, just next door to the Church Administration Building, right after President McKay died, and I assisted in notifying the other authorities. Just one of those experiences would have been the event of a lifetime!"

These men were not spared challenges. Elder Orson Hyde in an 1853 sermon spoke of the trials that come to those who do the Lord's work. He said, "It is invariably the case, that when an individual is ordained and appointed to lead the people, he has passed through tribulations and trials, and has proven himself before God, and before His people, that he is worthy of the situation which he holds." (*Journal of Discourses* 1:123.)

In 1957 Elder Spencer W. Kimball, diagnosed with cancer, went to a New York hospital for surgery on his throat. His close associate Elder Harold B. Lee counseled the physician, who was not a member of the Church, that this patient was no ordinary man, that the Lord had a work for Spencer Kimball to do. That he would lose his beautiful tenor singing voice was understood, but the doctor needed to preserve all he could of the larynx so Elder Kimball could continue to speak to the people. Following the surgery, Elder Kimball liked to joke that he had gone East and fallen among cutthroats. In later years, he did speak as president over the Church, with a raspy, easily recognized voice that eventually became so soft that a special microphone had to be attached to his glasses. "President Kimball knew much about sacrifice and suffering," states Arthur.

Arthur formed a bond with these men and with their counselors and associates. On Thanksgiving night, 1982, he received a call from President N. Eldon Tanner, first counselor to President Kimball. "Arthur, I got to thinking tonight about you," said President Tanner. "Did you have a good Thanksgiving? Did you have your family with you? How are they? How are you?"

Arthur recalls, "He was just like a kindly grandfather, and here he was a counselor in the First Presidency of the

Church with such weighty matters on his mind. I asked how he was, and he responded, 'A little shaky, a little tired.' "

Just before retiring to bed two hours later, Arthur received another call from the Tanner home. President Tanner had died shortly after their conversation. "He had genuine interest and compassion for me, a secretary," says Arthur. "That's the sort of men I worked with all those years."

Indeed, Arthur's experiences reinforced to him over and over that the Brethren have their feet on the ground. He adds: "They don't make hasty decisions. Members may sometimes ask, 'Why don't they do this? Why don't they do that?' But I tell you, they make haste very slowly and very deliberately and very prayerfully. They are righteous and sensitive." Arthur often reflects on the advice President J. Reuben Clark, a counselor to Presidents Grant, Smith, and McKay, gave newly called Church authorities: "Don't take yourself too seriously!"

Arthur learned to be flexible and cool-headed while he served in his secretarial positions. Over five decades he saw tremendous growth. Every program, stake organization, auxiliary, mission, handbook, and statistic changed dramatically from the beginning of his tenure. Arthur had no handbook on how to do his job, and training was limited; he usually followed himself in the position.

Each of the presidents had his own personality, and Arthur had to adapt to each one overnight. Looking back, he remembers the Church presidents like this: "President Heber J. Grant had tremendous fortitude and foresight. Anything he set his mind to do he accomplished, whether it was pitching baseball or financing Church projects. He was deeply committed to his people and their welfare in desperate times.

"President George Albert Smith was the most Christlike man I've ever known. He was gentle, kind, and totally devoted to mankind. He noticed only the good in others and was dedicated to organizations that helped develop strong character traits, like the Boy Scouts.

"President David O. McKay was tall and handsome. When he walked into the room it was just like electricity moving in every direction. Everybody's eyes turned in his direction, and he had the capacity to quickly touch people's hearts with his messages.

"President Joseph Fielding Smith was thoughtful, caring, and so very sensitive. He felt things so deeply and was easily touched by the littlest things. He had a sense of humor but he disliked having his picture taken, so I learned to place myself between him and any camera lens.

"None was more gracious, more hospitable, more capable or complex than President Harold B. Lee. He was always impeccably dressed, and he had an air about him that was inspirational. You could feel his presence in a small hall or a spacious auditorium.

"President Spencer W. Kimball had holes in his shoes—'worn out in the service of the Lord' he would say. He made time for everybody. When he was tired he would stretch out on his floor or his desk. He challenged the whole church to 'lengthen their stride' and in the process moved the work forward immeasurably.

"President Ezra Taft Benson is formal and very definite about the way he wants things done. He is sincere, kind, believing, and dedicated to the work. He was trained by the Lord with very individual experiences that have opened doors around the world and refocused attention on the Book of Mormon."

What impressed Arthur most about these men? These leaders who were focused on the enormous task of spreading the gospel to all mankind still found time to look after the individual, just as Christ did. They were generous with their time and their resources. Their busy schedules did not dictate their opportunities to serve. They had access to the whole Church system to get things done, and yet their contributions were often typical of the tools available to most: They listened, made calls, extended a helping hand and a willing heart, bore testimony of the gospel, and prayed for others.

Often Arthur was called on to give congratulations in behalf of the president for wedding anniversaries and birthdays. He answered volumes of letters. One little girl wrote asking the president to find a home for four little kittens. Two boys from Southern Utah wrote that their father was leaving their family, and they wondered what they could do. Mothers wrote, as did fathers, missionaries, and essentially anyone in the Church with something on his or her mind. Arthur would try to help, doing a little something here, a little something there.

Arthur describes the president's office as a solemn place: "People came with heavy hearts and burdens. I always felt that even if the answer was no, they had to go away feeling I had tipped the Church upside down to try to make it yes." He represented the president and was acting in his behalf, a responsibility he never took lightly.

Arthur witnessed hundreds of men and women called to key positions. "They didn't ask for these jobs. People in their right minds would never ask for one of these jobs. People know little of the demands that are made upon the leaders and their families, of the time and energy and strength required, and of the trials that come. It seems nice to be sitting up on the stand in the Tabernacle in big red chairs, but there is much more to it than that. I've sat with the leaders in meetings, and I know their hearts, their efforts and pressures, their great dedication and contributions."

Whenever a call was to be extended, Arthur had to devise some method to get the person in for an interview or on the phone without divulging the reason. It wasn't always easy. He has a story for almost every calling. A classic example is when President Joseph Fielding Smith called L. Tom Perry as a General Authority. Brother Perry, at the time a stake president in Boston, was coming to Salt Lake City for general conference, traveling by way of Arizona. Arthur missed him there but was told that Brother Perry's next stop was Brigham Young University, where he was going to see his son Lee. Arthur asked campus security to get Lee out of class, put him in the back of the police car, and wait at the entrance to the campus so he could point out his father when he passed. The plan worked, and the police stopped Brother Perry. Lee gave him the number to call. Arthur was waiting by the phone to set an appointment.

G. Homer Durham was tracked to a local mall, where he was walking for exercise with his wife when he was called as a member of the Quorum of the Seventy. Boyd K. Packer, an Assistant to the Twelve, was taken out of a meeting to be called as a member of the Council of the Twelve. Rex D. Pinegar, a mission president in West Virginia, was up in the hills, and Arthur tracked him all day before Brother Pinegar was near a phone and could be reached to return the call. Sister Michaelene P. Grassli, when called to the Primary General Presidency, was in a general board meeting, and the secretary said she'd give her the message to call. Arthur waited, called, and waited again, finally insisting she be interrupted and sent right over. She came.

Getting Elder Russell M. Nelson to a meeting with President Gordon B. Hinckley, counselor to President Kimball, was a memorable challenge for Arthur. Elder Marvin J. Ashton had taken ill in a conference session, and Brother Nelson, a renowned heart surgeon, had gone to the hospital to see that all was well. By phone he had reported the prognosis to President Hinckley, second counselor to President Kimball. But Arthur entreated him to go and talk to President Hinckley at his office at Church Headquarters. Brother Nelson questioned whether such a visit was necessary since he had relayed everything that he knew and President Hinckley kept such a full schedule. Arthur then suggested that President Hinckley had so many burdens that if Brother

Nelson could lift just this much from him it would make a big difference. After the interview, Elder Nelson, visibly shaken, said, "Why didn't you tell me?" Arthur usually saw these people right before they were called and then right after. "It was quite an experience to see this side of Church leadership," he says.

Arthur describes the presidents of the Church as diverse in talents, size, experience, age, and personality; however, in their understanding and application of the gospel they were equals. These were not men caught up in their own importance. "They knew this was the Lord's assignment, and they took it," says Arthur.

Arthur is articulate about the service of the Brethren he has witnessed over the years: "These men have been called by inspiration but they aren't perfect. There was only one perfect man, and he was crucified. He had his Judas. Others have had those who have betrayed them. There are always those who are willing to say things about the Brethren that are only partly true or taken out of context. But I know that the Lord loves the Brethren. He has had them in his watch-care since they were born. He upholds them, sustains them, reveals his mind and will to them. He has called them to the work, and he magnifies and blesses them, and they lead under his counsel.

"These men leading the Church have broad responsibilities, but their testimonies are simple. President Clark advised the Saints more than fifty years ago, 'Believe that Jesus is the Christ, the head of this church, and that Joseph Smith is a prophet of God, that he saw and heard what he said he did.' Such testimonies speak of the expressions of faith of the members all over the world."

Says Arthur, who has met members everywhere, "No matter the language, the Saints know that God lives and that Jesus Christ, our Elder Brother, leads this church through a prophet on the earth. That conviction is in essence the strength of the Church today. Relying on that strength, the presidents of the Church and the other General Authorities direct the work forward."

Arthur has spent a lifetime with these presidents, their families, and their friends. He knows them as few other people do. He knows their hearts, their efforts, their problems, their convictions. He knows of their dedication and their untiring efforts to build the kingdom. "The General Authorities spend every ounce of energy, strength, and talent with which the Lord has blessed them to uplift the members and good people everywhere. That is their special assignment," says Arthur.

"I've laughed with them, I've cried with them, I've prayed with them, I've traveled with them, I've worked at their side," Arthur says. "I have great love and admiration for these men of God."

Arthur has watched at close range as the prophets have guided the work forward. His memories, many presented in this book, are of the diligence, charity, kindness, humility, and love of these seven presidents of the Church. Arthur has been in many sensitive sessions where weighty matters were discussed. He has known of changes before official announcements were made, and he was often the first to embrace a newly called leader. But his treasured recollections are of the warm handshakes, the quiet moments in sacred settings, the personal lessons learned in everyday activities, and the chance to follow the Lord's anointed in their teachings, their example, and their counsel.

He has been with Saints all over the world as they have sung "We Thank Thee, O God, for a Prophet." But it is the phrase "to guide us in these latter days" to which he gives the greatest significance when he says, "I can testify that if we follow the prophets, we will never get on forbidden paths. They are the Lord's servants and his mouthpieces upon the earth in these latter days."

CHAPTER ONE

D. Arthur Haycock: Prepared to Serve

Being able to take shorthand opened doors for D. Arthur Haycock and secured for him employment at the Church Offices in 1938. But those skills didn't come easy. As a student at South High School, he failed shorthand his first year in the course. "Your loops are too large," the teacher said. "Your figures are too irregular." Arthur could read his notes easily, but he enrolled again in the course for a second year and, under the tutelage of a new teacher, finished at the top of the class.

He hadn't always been interested in office work—but he had always worked. In his youth he labored in the fields topping beets and harvesting potatoes. Later, he and his brother had a paper route after school while his school chums cheered at football games and practiced for plays. He delivered packages in the summer for Keith O'Brien and the Paris Company department stores in Salt Lake City. The Haycock children supplemented the family income doing odd jobs at a very early age.

The oldest of four children, Arthur was born September 4, 1916, in Farmington, Utah. He was blessed with the first name *David* for his father and *Arthur* for his mother's brother; the blessing took place at the old rock meetinghouse in Farmington where the first Primary was organized. His father had emigrated to Zion with his family from Staffordshire, England, when only a baby. His mother, Lily Crane

Haycock, was born in Herriman, Utah, a small community in the Salt Lake Valley.

The Haycocks settled in Bancroft, Idaho, when Arthur was small. As an infant and toddler, he had many close calls with death. As a baby, he nearly suffocated in his buggy but was rescued by his mother and a friend when he was already blue and not breathing. At three, while fetching some water, he dropped his bucket through a small hole in a bridge and slipped, falling headfirst into the canal below. His mother found him just in time, with his feet kicking wildly in the air.

Shortly after the incident, an aunt and uncle came to visit. A mechanic, his uncle offered to overhaul the Haycocks' car. Arthur appointed himself first assistant and in the process smeared his overalls with grease and gasoline. They were his only overalls, so he slipped them on again the next day. Playing outside with his friends, Arthur and the little group were playing with matches when one fell into his lap, and his clothes burst into flames. Instinctively Arthur hunched over to protect his face and started screaming. His uncle and mother came racing from inside, wrapped him in a blanket to extinguish the flames, and rushed him to the country doctor. Equipment and medical supplies were limited, and he was burned severely on his abdomen and his right thigh. With Arthur sedated by chloroform, the doctor scraped off the dead flesh. The boy's heart stopped during the operation; the doctor revived him. His arduous recovery was accompanied by periods of intense pain.

Arthur's right leg pulled up close to his body as the burn healed, and soon he could not straighten it. The muscles had contracted, and to extend the leg to its normal position was impossible, so the doctor decided to straighten it gradually over several months. With the help of the boy's parents, the doctor would press down on the leg, extending it about a quarter of an inch, and then bandage it in the new position. The process was eventually successful, and Arthur regained

2

the use of his leg. Still, for six months, David, his father, carried him around on a pillow after the bandages were removed. Because of the accident, Arthur's right leg was always shorter than his left, though he disguised the limp well, wearing out his shoes unevenly. His mother, and later his wife, were able to distinguish his footsteps by his noticeable gait.

By the time Arthur was back on his feet, his father had been called on a mission to the Northern States. The family, now including younger brother Gordon and a baby sister, Donna Jeanette, moved from Idaho back to Herriman to be near their mother's family.

The Haycocks struggled for sufficient food and necessities. Arthur recalls not wanting to finish his scrambled eggs one morning. Waiting until his mother wasn't looking, he ran outside and dumped the food. When his mother came back, she asked if he'd finished his breakfast. Unable to lie, he told her he hadn't and that it was out on the ashes from the stove. She sent him to retrieve the morsels and then watched as he scraped off the ashes and finished his breakfast.

During those years Arthur herded cows, harvested potatoes, pulled weeds, gathered firewood in the canyon, and later hauled hay to help the family survive. The young family moved repeatedly as they searched for more reasonable accommodations. None of the places provided much comfort. Just before Arthur's father was to be released from his mission, Grandfather Haycock, a painter and paperhanger in Nephi, fell and died from the injuries. David was allowed to return home from his mission about a month early for the funeral.

Reunited, the family moved to Firth, Idaho, in the fall of 1924, a community Arthur remembers as hostile to Mormons. At first, the Haycocks rented the residence of the Baptist minister, a rather nice house with indoor plumbing, the first Arthur had seen. The luxury did not last long, for they were forced soon to find a smaller, less expensive home.

Arthur's father, a barber, worked in the one barbershop in town. Located in the largest building on the main street, the barbershop shared the facility with the movie theater, the grocery store, and a meat market. Upstairs was a roller rink and a dance hall. To add to the family coffers, Arthur was soon sweeping out the movie theater; his mother played the piano to accompany the silent films. She played soft, sweet music for tender scenes and military or melancholy music for others.

The Haycocks were recognized as stalwart Mormons in the community. Arthur was baptized in a canal and ordained a deacon while in Firth. They attended meetings on the second floor over the mercantile store. In the winter, the room was heated by a pot-bellied stove that was only marginally effective. Snow drifts sometimes reached thirty feet high, making it possible for Arthur to touch the telephone wires on his way to school.

In the summer of 1929, the family returned to Utah, settling in Salt Lake City in the Liberty Ward, not far from the downtown area. Arthur attended South Junior High on 1300 South and State Street. Used to a four-room school with two grades in each class, he got lost the first day in the spacious building of a dozen rooms.

The Haycocks returned just in time for the Great Depression, which hit in October. Purchasing another barber shop at 1118 South West Temple, three blocks from their house, Arthur's father struggled during those years, earning about sixty dollars a month. Joining ROTC, which subsidized the purchase of school books, and taking summer jobs, Arthur contributed to the family income. While Arthur was at South Junior High, typing became one of his best subjects. When he advanced to the new South High School, one of the students in its first class, Arthur determined to expand such skills. South High was a two-year high school that offered students the option of a third year of postgraduate courses.

Arthur chose to continue his education at South after graduating, and he took such commercial and business subjects as dictation, transcription, and bookkeeping. When he completed his courses, he could take dictation at 140 words a minute.

Certainly his school courses prepared him for his work. But his schooling also brought him in contact with a young seminary instructor, Harold B. Lee, who later became the eleventh president of the Church with Arthur as his secretary.

Arthur graduated from high school in a pair of $.98 white pants, his worn navy coat, and a $1.98 pair of white shoes with rubber soles. Ready to play a greater part in helping support the family, he joined the Civilian Conservation Corps quartered at Fort Douglas on Salt Lake City's east bench. Finding a uniform small enough to fit his frame had been difficult in ROTC, and the CCC faced the same challenge. Arthur worked in the warehouse, writing supply and food orders for thirty camps in the western United States. He was paid thirty dollars a month; he kept five dollars and sent the rest to his parents.

While serving with the CCC, Arthur received a mission call to Hawaii. He left the end of April 1935, arriving in Honolulu by ocean liner on May 5, four months before his nineteenth birthday. He would later return to the islands at different times with six of the presidents of the Church, serve there as a mission president, and serve as president of the Hawaii Temple.

Arthur's first experience in the mission field was not what he had expected. His companion took him on the streetcar to the end of the line, and then the two walked up to the top of a hill. Perplexed, Arthur could see no homes for tracting or people for teaching. That's when his companion stretched out in the tall grass and napped most of the day. Arthur read his scriptures to keep occupied and finally slept as well. "It was not what I expected," he later recalled, "and

5

I have counseled missionaries and their leaders all over the world to give the finest companions to new elders so that they can get the spirit of the work immediately."

In spite of such experiences, his heart was in the work, and it stayed there. When the Hawaiian mission was organized as a stake, a major step for the Church since it was the first one outside the continental United States, Arthur was serving his mission.

President and Sister Heber J. Grant, President and Sister J. Reuben Clark, and Joseph Anderson, secretary to President Grant, arrived by boat in June 1935 to establish the stake. When President Grant and his associates traveled from Oahu to Kauai, Arthur joined them on the journey since he had been transferred to that island.

While he was on his mission, Arthur identified what he wanted to do with his skills and his life. He recalls being impressed with the activity and dedication of Joseph Anderson. He says, "I observed Joseph Anderson at work and made up my mind that I wanted that kind of job. Lacking education and contacts, it was only a dream."

Arthur served as secretary and stenographer in the mission home, his first taste of coordinating and keeping things organized in an office. He was later transferred to the big island of Hawaii to replace an elder who had contracted typhoid fever. Arthur and his companion walked everywhere, often more than thirty miles a day. To lessen the monotony between destinations, the elders practiced their Hawaiian. They lived in a small, one-room shanty attached to the side of the chapel. Backing onto the jungle, the place was rat infested and lacked all comforts. To shower, the elders stood under an old, wooden ice-cream tub with holes punched in the bottom to dispense their water—the rain.

The elders, who were called on to bless the sick, conduct meetings, and perform baptisms and special services, set out one day for a thirty-five-mile trek to the north end of the Kona territory to perform a marriage. Having had no

6

breakfast, they nibbled on wild berries as they made their way toward the ranch. They hitched a ride for a five-mile stretch.

Originally they had hoped to stay with the branch president and his wife, but they received word that the wife had just delivered a new baby. They felt their arrival would be an imposition, so they had decided to stay with a Hawaiian sister whose meager resources forced her to live on sour poi and cold rice. The missionaries were not excited about the prospects.

Still, they trudged on. As they started across a massive lava-flow desert, a storm loomed in the distance. They watched as it moved closer and closer. The lava flow terrain provided no shelter, and they were forced to tramp through the rain, soaked to the skin. To keep up their spirits, they mused about their favorite foods, what they would eat right now if they could choose the perfect meal. The two missionaries, short Arthur and his gangly companion towering above him, settled on thick slices of bacon with fresh eggs fried in the grease.

When the storm hit, the branch president had gone out in his truck looking for the elders. He eventually found them, cold and weary, and took them to his home. While they were showering and changing into borrowed dry clothes, he fixed them dinner. Not knowing of their tastes but anticipating healthy appetites, he quickly slaughtered a wild boar he had killed in the mountains that day and fried the pork with fresh eggs. It was a testimony to Arthur that "the Lord looks after his servants if they will do their part."

Released from his mission in June 1937, Arthur was met at the boat in San Francisco by his parents and his sweetheart, Maurine McClellan. The two were married May 6, 1938, in the Salt Lake Temple. Then Arthur went to work at a Salt Lake hotel for ten dollars a week writing letters for hotel guests. He took dictation for messages to business associates, friends, or families and prepared final letters for the guests to mail. Then he changed jobs and went to work for the *Salt Lake Tribune* information desk for eighteen dollars a week. His job was to answer questions for those who phoned the desk and to give out sports scores.

With some time for dreaming, Arthur remembered President Heber J. Grant's visit to the Hawaiian mission and the activity of his able secretary, Joseph Anderson. Arthur determined to pursue a post at the Church offices, and every Monday on his lunch hour he walked two blocks to the headquarters to apply for a job. His persistence paid off. After six months he was offered a position in the Finance Department at $100 a month. That same day, he also received an offer from the FBI to become a special agent at a salary of $150 a month. But, he says, "my heart was with the Church and its work." He was delighted with the prospects of his new employment.

The Haycocks blessed their first daughter, Marilyn, on Sunday, September 3, 1939, the day Britain declared war on Germany for its incursion into Poland. Arthur was required to register for the draft, but his age and family status exempted him from an immediate call to military service. By 1941 tensions in the world had escalated, and the day the Haycocks blessed their second daughter, Judy, on December 7, 1941, Japan bombed Pearl Harbor.

Since Arthur was registered for the draft, he was advised that he could not remain in an office but would have to go to work in some war-related activity, either the mines, the smelter, or the railroad. He chose the railroad, as had fellow Church employee Gordon B. Hinckley. Dressed in overalls, blue work shirt, gloves, and a red bandanna, with his feet protected by steel-toed boots, Arthur reported for work in the Rio Grande shops and helped repair steam engines for 68 cents an hour. No dictation was taken here. The work was gruelling and dangerous, particularly for Arthur, who weighed only 119 pounds. But he knew how to work and soon advanced to the machine shop, where the employees repaired parts for the big engines. When the stationmaster, Gordon Hinckley, was transferred to the Denver headquarters, Arthur was offered his job, complete with a blue suit, brass buttons, and conductor's cap. He was responsible for the supervision of the station twenty-four hours a day with the help of two assistants. By the time the war had ended in Europe and the focus had shifted to Japan in the summer of 1945, Arthur was allowed to return to Church employment when he was recruited by Richard L. Evans to serve as office manager of the *Improvement Era* in 1945. Though he had an obvious future at the railroad, his interest was still with the growing Church. Little did he know it was just the beginning of decades of service.

Heber J. Grant

Heber J. Grant was called as president of the Church two years after Arthur was born. In 1938, when Arthur began his Church employment, President Grant had been steering the Church for twenty years, bringing it through the Great Depression, getting it out of debt, and starting the welfare program.

The office arrangement at 47 East South Temple when Arthur began work there in 1938 was far less formal than it is today. The Finance Department, where he worked, occupied a large room on the main floor that was divided only by desks and files. President Grant would come through the office every day and hold an informal meeting to discuss financial issues with the supervisors. He always shook hands with everyone he passed, spoke to staff members, and showed genuine interest in their experiences and daily lives.

Not long after Arthur started in the Church offices, President Grant stopped at his desk on the way to a meeting with his counselors. Over six feet tall, he towered over Arthur's five-foot-six frame. A great patron of the arts in Utah, he asked Arthur if he would like to choose a painting for his home from his private collection. President Grant invited Arthur to follow him up to his private office on the fourth floor. All the office walls were covered with original oil paintings and watercolors by such artists as John Hafen,

President Heber J. Grant and his wife, Augusta Winters Grant

Joseph A. F. Everett, and James T. Harwood—artists whose names were becoming known for exceptional skill and mastery. Arthur recalls, "It was a gallery like no other in town." President Grant urged the newly married clerk to take his pick. Arthur's mind quickly flashed to his modest two-room apartment with little furniture and what a surprise was in store for his wife. After studying each picture, he picked out a watercolor by Everett titled "Autumn Grandeur," which depicted the east mountains of the Salt Lake Valley in the fall. President Grant, in his elegant handwriting, autographed the back of the painting for his finance clerk and dated the gift, May 15, 1942. The picture has hung in the Haycocks' living room for fifty years.

President Grant was known for his generosity. To help young artists finance their early careers, he had his daughters take painting lessons from them. He also purchased many of their works, which hung in his office until he gave them to friends and associates. The president often gave away books. Arthur recalls that missionaries, children, visitors from out of town, and others who met with President Grant invariably left the Church office building with a new book in their hands. The gift's value was enhanced by the signature of President Grant on the inside. His distinctive penmanship was a result of practice and dedication. Arthur learned to value these traits as he saw how President Grant had used them so effectively in his own life. "What I learned from the presidents," says Arthur, "is that this life is a testing ground to make each of us strong and effective. Their example was always the right example." President Grant gave his time as well as his means. For years he took groups of widows of General Authorities for rides up the canyon to see spring flowers or autumn leaves.

President Grant often told congregations of his efforts to achieve. He gave missionaries cards with quotations and poems that suggested effort, drive, determination in reaching their goals. He often told congregations of his own efforts to focus and achieve. When he was young he wanted to become a great baseball pitcher. He hung a peach basket on the barn door and threw the ball into that target day after day until he was successful ninety-eight out of one hundred times. He became the pitcher for the high-school baseball team and won the state championship. While serving as president of the Church, he decided to take voice lessons. When he visited the Hawaiian Islands in 1935, one of the Saints reported that when President Grant left by boat for the big island of Hawaii, the people gathered at the dock and sang "Come, Come Ye Saints." Even though his boat was fast leaving the port, President Grant sang with them as loud as he could until those gathered could no longer see him.

Definite in his opinions, President Grant would take a position and stick to it. Arthur remembers being in the Presidency's office when President Grant, President Clark, and President McKay were discussing calling someone to a par-

The First Presidency on the east side of the Church Administration Building: J. Reuben Clark, Heber J. Grant, and David O. McKay

ticular position. President Grant said bluntly, "I don't know about that fellow." The other two were much in favor of him. President Grant continued, "No, he's stubborn; he's so stubborn that if he drowned in the Ogden River, he'd float upstream. We just have to get someone else."

President Grant was a man of decision. His resolute nature helped him guide the Church through the Great Depression. When financial institutions were collapsing across the country, he helped the Church keep its financial enterprises together. When banks were failing in 1929, the people lined up a block away from a Church-owned bank to get their money. The bank met each request. Most of the people redeposited their funds once they realized that the accounts were covered.

For Arthur, employment at the Church headquarters was all he had imagined. He walked to work from his home on First North, just a few blocks from the offices, and often ran into President McKay on the way. "I idolized him and the others," says Arthur. "I watched how hard they worked and how sincere they were. I had never seen such dedication. These were giants in aging bodies, men like Rudger Clawson, James E. Talmage, Melvin J. Ballard, Reed Smoot, John A. Widtsoe, and Charles A. Callis."

At first President Clark seemed remote. But as Arthur worked with him, he recognized this former State Department official and U.S. Ambassador to Mexico as a highly sensitive manager. He often said to Arthur, "I have had a hundred secretaries all over the world, and you are the finest."

During President Grant's tenure, only two secretaries, Pearl Johnson and Jeannette Hanks, worked for the Brethren, doing all the correspondence for the Council of the Twelve. Arthur observed that each of the Church leaders had a specific style of operation. For example, Elder Talmage became a little frustrated with the office staff one day when they could not find a certain letter that had been filed. He was so particular that he dictated every comma, colon, and semicolon. The secretaries finally suggested they make him another copy, which brought the reply, "I don't want another copy. I want that copy. I'm not so concerned about that being lost but that anything could be lost in our offices." They finally found the missing document—in the wastebasket.

The Church authorities were practical men. While their work was focused on the gospel, they understood day-to-day living in very pragmatic terms. When Arthur was faced with having to leave Church employment and take a job related to the war effort, he sought advice about what job to take. Elder Harold B. Lee counseled him, "I've found in this world, if you don't look out for yourself, no one else will."

Near the end of his life, President Grant's health began to fail following a slight stroke he suffered while he was in California at a Church conference. Weeks later Arthur was walking through the Onyx Room on the first floor of the Church Office Building when he saw President Grant sitting on the couch, squeezing a rubber ball in his right hand as part of his therapy to regain its full use. When Arthur went to shake his hand, President Grant extended his left hand. Arthur recalls, "There were tears in his eyes as he said, 'Well, they say I haven't had a stroke. But if I haven't, I surely did have its first cousin.' " That was the last time the two talked. President Grant died May 14, 1945.

CHAPTER THREE

George Albert Smith

In 1947, two years after George Albert Smith began serving as president of the Church, the Church celebrated its centennial year. The commemoration of the arrival of the pioneers in the Salt Lake Valley included the dedication of the This Is the Place Monument and numerous other significant sites, the issuance of a centennial stamp, the traditional parade on July 24, a spiritual pageant ("The Message of the Ages") presented in the Tabernacle, a Scout jamboree at East High School, a recreation of the pioneer trek by the Sons of the Utah Pioneers, an exposition at the fairgrounds, and the presentation of a musical, *Promised Valley*. More than 185,000 people visited Temple Square during July of 1947. It was a season of grand events and tributes.

Joseph Anderson had served as secretary to both the president of the Church and the First Presidency since 1922, but the growing demands of the job necessitated getting additional help. Arthur had been working on the staff of the *Improvement Era*, but he was "loaned" to President Smith, ostensibly to help with the centennial activities. However, working in the president's office, Arthur soon realized he was being "checked out" for a permanent position. After two weeks, the magazine was notified to get someone else; Arthur had a new job.

To tell the story of the Latter-day Saints settling Zion, President Smith participated in a radio broadcast on the

*D. Arthur Haycock
and Joseph Anderson*

NBC network on the topic "The Rise of the New West," saying, "Unlike most other westward-bound emigrants of the time, these pioneers came not for wealth, but to create homes where they could worship God unmolested. . . . Bound by recognized ties of brotherhood and guided by Christian ideals, which were part of their very fiber, they knew how to live and work together without suppressing individualism." (*Church News*, July 26, 1947, pp. 1, 10.)

President Smith held a great reverence for his heritage. A member of the Mayflower Society, the Sons of the American Revolution, and the Sons of the Utah Pioneers, he had spearheaded the building of This Is the Place Monument at the mouth of Emigration Canyon to commemorate the trek of the Mormon pioneers. "Dedicating that statue was one of the pinnacles of his personal life," says Arthur.

In the dedicatory prayer, President Smith said, "While we dedicate this monument of stone, and while it has been embellished by the figures of thy children, we realize that these are all now at peace with one another. How can we,

Heavenly Father, as we live in the world and enjoy the influence of thy Spirit, fail to be at peace with one another? Grant that we may remember the advice and counsel of thy Son when he was upon the earth, that we should love our neighbor as ourselves." (*Improvement Era,* September 1947, p. 571.)

World War II had recently ended, lights had started coming on all over the world, and the need for a great deal of healing was apparent during this period. "It was George Albert Smith's finest hour," Arthur says. "Here was a man who was as Christ-like as anyone who ever lived. Kind and gentle, he was a friend to everyone."

Named for his grandfather, George A. Smith, counselor to Brigham Young and cousin of the Prophet Joseph Smith, President George Albert Smith had been significantly influenced by his family's contributions to the Church. "I know you appreciate the deep reverence I have in my soul for my own forebears," he would say as he took visitors to the window of his office in the northeast corner of Church headquarters and point out Ensign Peak. "Look at that peak with its clumps of foliage and bare land," he would say. "That's how the valley looked when my grandfather came here. There's no place in the world where you're more welcome than you are here."

As secretary to the president, Arthur did much more than office work. A daily companion to President George Albert Smith, he drove him home at night and anywhere he needed to go during the day. In those days there was no underground walkway from the Church Administration Building to Temple Square. Usually Arthur drove the president, and often his counselors, to the temple or the Tabernacle and would have the car waiting to take them back to their offices.

To get to Temple Square from the Church offices, Arthur had to drive a circuitous route. A narrow, one-way road cut through the Church offices block, but it ran east, away from Temple Square. Arthur would pick up his passengers behind

President George Albert Smith in his office at the Church Administration Building

the Church Administration Building and drive them almost around the block, back to the north entrance to Temple Square. "It was a rather roundabout route, but nevertheless the legal way to go," Arthur says.

One cold winter morning, with President Smith in the front seat and Presidents David O. McKay and J. Reuben Clark in the back, President Smith instructed Arthur to take a more direct route and go west instead of east. The guard at the entrance to the private road came running out of his station, blowing his whistle and waving his arms. Arthur ignored him. A few minutes later when Arthur came back with his empty car, the guard was waiting for him. "Didn't you hear my whistle?" he yelled. "Why didn't you stop? Don't you know you were going the wrong way on a one-way street?"

Arthur explained that the Presidency was late for their temple meeting. When that didn't seem to smooth over the infraction, he looked at the guard and said, "Well, the president of the Church told me to go that way and so I did. And

19

if he tells me to drive this car up the steps of the Church Administration Building, that's where it's going."

Arthur was totally loyal. "I had to see and not see, hear and not hear," he explains. "I had to be aware of everything that was happening so I could help the president in any way necessary. But I was keenly aware I was just there to help."

Arthur watched President George Albert Smith's constant service to the people. It was clear that he made friends with everybody, and they weren't just casual acquaintances. His "hope to see you again," was no superficial parting remark; he meant it. His sincerity always came through whether he was writing to a head of state or to his grandchildren. When he met people or made new friends, he would have Arthur add their names and addresses to his list of correspondents and would sometimes keep in touch with them the rest of his life. He met the Queen of Tonga on a tour in 1938, and the two corresponded until she died. When her son became the king, President Smith wrote to him. That was his pattern. He traveled more than a million miles around the world in the interest of the gospel of Jesus Christ. "Wherever I have gone," he wrote in 1950, "I have found noble men and women." (*Improvement Era*, April 1950, p. 263.)

A sunstroke President Smith suffered while doing survey work at the University of Utah in 1918 had left him with only one "good" eye. Arthur read him his mail and took dictation for his letters. "In much of his correspondence, I saw him lift burdens from the shoulders of others and put them on his own," Arthur says. "If there ever was a man who consciously spread the balm of Gilead, it was George Albert Smith."

The two were going through the mail one day when Arthur burst out laughing. President Smith sat patiently and waited for him to quiet down. "What in the world was in that letter?" he asked.

Arthur told him, "There's a good soul who wants to

know what your feeling is on cocoa and cremation. I can't think of two less related subjects." President Smith shot back, "Write and tell him they're both hot."

Arthur learned quickly that President Smith rarely got angry, "but," Arthur says, "he couldn't abide a man whose wife had put him through school only to be replaced by a girl at the office whose hair was always in place." This happened with a family that was very close to him, and though he made a special trip to Nevada to dissuade the man from leaving his family, he came back unsuccessful. "I never heard him curse," says Arthur, "but if he was going to really take after someone (like this fellow), he'd call him a 'first-class scrub.' That was the worst thing he would say about anybody."

President Smith enjoyed having someone to talk to, and Arthur had a good listening ear. In particular, President Smith liked to talk about growing up in Salt Lake City just blocks from Temple Square.

In his childhood, everyone in town had a little garden behind the house and a shed with a cow, and in the front there was a dirt sidewalk with an irrigation ditch by its side. All the neighbors took turns irrigating, starting at three o'clock in the morning. President Smith said the water in that ditch was just about the best water on earth. He would lean down on his hands and knees and take big, long drinks. One Sabbath he was a little late for Sunday School. He was drinking from the ditch when he noticed a shiny object on the bank in the grass. Curious, he reached down and picked it up. It was an empty 30–30 cartridge shell. Not sure what to do with it, he stuffed the shell into his pocket and hurried off to church. The children sat on the benches with their teachers. In that era the prayers were long; so were the talks and the songs. Ten-year-old George Albert was pretty restless by the time they got to the sacrament. That's when he remembered the shell in his pocket and wondered what he could do with it, thinking maybe he could trade it for some

21

marbles. The boy next to him suggested that he use it for a whistle, which he promptly did. Puffing up his cheeks, he blew as hard as he could, and he was eminently successful. Chuckling, President Smith told Arthur, "It's been seventy years since that happened, and the teacher hasn't given back that cartridge shell yet."

Sometimes President Smith described feeling inadequate when at age thirty-three he was called to the Council of the Twelve Apostles. It was when he overheard two drunks discussing his appointment that he finally came to terms with the call. Quipped one, "I think it's more relation than revelation." The other responded, "Have you ever considered that the Lord doesn't care what you or anybody else thinks?"

But President Smith struggled with more than just the magnitude of his call. For many years he thought that his poor health hampered his ability to fulfill his calling—that the Lord had called him to work, not to be ill. He went to St. George and lived in a tent for a summer, hoping the desert climate would restore his strength. Says Arthur, "President Smith felt if he couldn't be well and do the Lord's work, he wanted the Lord to get someone else who could."

While lying on his sickbed in St. George, he dreamed he got out of a boat on the shore of a beautiful lake and began walking along a path that led to a grove of trees. His grandfather, George A. Smith, emerged from the woods and recognized his grandson, and the two hurried to each other and embraced. His grandfather weighed more than 300 pounds; George Albert only 155. His venerable grandfather said, "I've come to see what you've done with my name." At that moment, President Smith saw his whole life pass before him, and he said, "Grandfather, I have done nothing with your name of which you need be ashamed." President Smith often described the experience as a major turning point in his life. He put his health concerns aside and went back to work.

In 1948 he told those gathered at general conference,

"After having traveled approximately a million miles in the world in the interest of the gospel of Jesus Christ, one of the frailest of my mother's eleven children, I testify that the Lord has preserved my life, and I have had joy beyond expression, and I have enjoyed the results of loving my neighbors as myself and all this brings happiness."

Over the years President Smith developed a dramatic sense of purpose and integrity. If President Smith said something, that's what he meant. "You could trust him completely," says Arthur. "You could expect that his actions were in concert with the gospel." President Smith talked about such dedication with others when he said, "You put me in jail and I would always look for an opportunity to escape. But if you put me in a room with doors and windows, unbarred and unguarded, and you draw a line and ask for my promise that I will never try to escape, I'll never step across that line."

President Smith was born and reared in the LDS Seventeenth Ward, one of the original nineteen wards in the valley. His home was located on West Temple Street, just down the block from the home of Church President Wilford Woodruff. The Smith and Woodruff families were close, and George Albert was particularly interested in the Woodruffs' granddaughter Lucy. Arthur recalls hearing President Smith reminisce about those years in his youth when Lucy would walk by his house on the way to her aunt's house to get potato water to make yeast. "He often went out and chased her," says Arthur. In school he sat behind her and dipped her pigtails in the inkwell because he liked her and wanted to get her attention.

One day George Albert and Lucy were sitting on the porch swing watching a crowd outside a rooming house for traveling salesmen, the current site of the Inn on Temple Square. One of the guests had made a small hot-air balloon out of a tin can, a handkerchief, and a candle. The invention was floating toward Temple Square when George Albert

exclaimed, "Lucy, that is going to hit the roof of the Tabernacle." Sure enough, it did. The candle tipped over, and the
Tabernacle's wooden shingles caught fire. George Albert
rushed to the rooming house to call the fire department, and
the fire fighters came charging up with their horses snorting.
Arriving at the west entrance of Temple Square, they found
the wooden gates locked. The fire chief instructed his men
and the boys who had gathered around to run as fast as they
could, leap, and plant their feet high on the gate. Their force
knocked it down. The fire engine pulled up to the Tabernacle, and the fire fighters extinguished the flames before the
roof was badly damaged.

George Albert used to take Lucy for rides in his father's
buggy. Other suitors were also pursuing her, including one
who used his father's brand new Studebaker buggy with
leather interior and red wheels to put on quite a campaign.
In the midst of it all, George Albert got his mission call to the
Southern States, where J. Golden Kimball was serving as
president. Going over to see Lucy and bid her farewell,
George Albert realized she'd probably be married to someone else before his return. "I just wanted to say good-bye,"
he told her. Her reply surprised him: "George Albert Smith,
if you think you're going to the Southern States without me,
you're wrong. Let's get married and go together." They did.

President Smith and Arthur attended the 100th anniversary celebration of the Seventeenth Ward, where President
Smith had grown up. The Haycocks had also lived in the
ward when they were first married. Arthur describes the
wonderful reunion: "Here was this local boy who was now
serving as president of the Church. The people were all generous with their handshakes and warm wishes. At the end of
the evening's commemoration, I slipped out of the chapel to
get his overcoat. When I returned, I saw him leaning over,
listening to a tiny girl about five years old. She was whis-
pering, he was smiling, and her parents were trying to hurry

her along. After she left, I helped him on with his coat, and we left with no further conversation."

The next morning as Arthur was reading President Smith his mail, the prophet leaned back in his chair and said how wonderful it was to go back to the ward of his youth and see so many of his friends. Then he looked at his secretary and asked, "Did you see that little girl and hear what she said when she tugged on my coat? She wanted to tell me something, so I leaned down and she whispered in my ear, 'President Smith, I love you.' Of all the wonderful things said and the friends I saw, that was the sweetest thing that happened."

Looking back on that discussion, Arthur says, "That little girl felt the spirit of the moment, and she sensed that here was her friend and she just had to express it. The incident reminded me of the song in Primary that no doubt this little girl knew: 'I think when I read that sweet story of old, when Jesus was here among men, how he called little children like lambs to his fold. I should like to have been with him then.' "

In his counsel to the Saints, President Smith was precise. To a crowd of BYU students on the Provo campus in October 1948 he said, "One of our difficulties in this world today is that too many of our Father's children do not believe in God. They have an idea that they can do just as they please and they throw their lives away. . . . The [pathway] of righteousness is the highway of happiness." (*Church News*, October 20, 1948, p. 2-c.)

That Arthur had skills in shorthand initially opened the door for his longtime secretarial position. At a conference in Denver with President Smith, he became intrigued with a new electronic recording device developed for use in court reporting. It used two wax cylinders; when the one cylinder got near the end, the other would automatically start recording so that there was a two-minute overlap, ensuring that none of the proceedings were lost. Arthur was used to

*D. Arthur Haycock with
his stenographer's pad,
about 1947*

a less sophisticated system. Delighted with the opportunity to try the new machine, Arthur put his dictation book into his pocket and watched, entranced, as the new invention did his work. When the two were in the car heading for the train station, President Smith turned to Arthur and said, "Well, did I speak too fast for you tonight?"

Arthur replied, "No, President, I got along just fine. As a matter of fact I quit altogether. The stake president had an incredible new machine to take down your talk, so there was no need for me to fuss with taking down the service in shorthand."

President Smith nodded and said, "I noticed that. I got to

thinking what would have happened if the electricity had gone off, or if they had dropped the wax cylinder, or if it was cracked or just didn't work. You know, Arthur, I have always figured it's better to have the notes and not need them than to need them and not have them."

After this gentle reminder of Arthur's responsibility, he took everything down in shorthand, no matter how many recording machines were in operation.

Arthur was valuable not only for his dictation; he also knew his way around the railroad, from timetables to private cars. He and President Smith logged thousands of miles together and in the process met with bankers and business executives, church and community leaders.

President Heber J. Grant had increased the Church's visibility with his participation on boards of directors, talks given at various events, and association with many great financiers. President George Albert Smith continued the involvement. At the invitation of railroad officials, he always traveled in a private rail car, often the personal car of the president of the railroad. He enjoyed chatting with the stewards on the rail lines and had a funny habit of calling all of them "Bill," whether that was their name or not.

The Brethren usually traveled by train if their assignments took them long distances. In those years right after the war, the General Authorities rarely used the airlines, and they sometimes took their cars. But President Smith loved to fly. During the Depression he had flown in an open-cockpit plane, sitting on a mailbag, on one of the first flights to Las Vegas and then on to Los Angeles. Whenever he had assignments that gave him the chance, he'd take the plane.

President Smith served on the board of Western Airlines. While Arthur usually traveled with him, on one occasion President Smith flew to California alone. The next morning after he returned, while reviewing with Arthur the appointments for the day, President Smith sat back in his chair and closed his eyes. "I had an interesting experience flying home last night," he said. "It was foggy in Los Angeles when we took off. I thought we'd get above it, but we didn't and I was concerned. I knew we had some high mountains to get over; I just didn't know if we could.

"Being an officer of the company, I went up to the front to talk to the pilot, and I asked him, 'How do you know where you are going? How high are we? You have all these instruments, but how do you know you are on the right direction for Salt Lake?'

"The pilot told me that he wore his earphones to receive a signal that he would follow. He said that if he got off course to the right, he would hear dot-dot-dot. If he got off course to the left, he would hear dash-dash-dash. If he heard a steady signal, he knew he was right on course."

President Smith asked the pilot, "Are you sure your altimeter is all right?"

The pilot nodded, "Yes."

In a few minutes, the pilot set the plane down without a bump at the Salt Lake City airport.

Then President Smith told Arthur, "I've been thinking about that experience. I've likened that plane to the Church. The passengers are the members, and the pilot is the president. That pilot had earphones on, and he could hear the signals, but I couldn't hear anything. I could have gotten a parachute and jumped out over Nevada and landed on a cactus in the desert, but I decided to stay with the plane. I've concluded that if the people of the Church, the passengers, will stay with the plane and have confidence in the pilot, the prophet, who has on the earphones, who gets the messages and knows where they come from, they'll land safely as well." President Smith summed up the experience: "The prophet of the Church hears the message, and he knows the source."

To Arthur, such discussions were never commonplace: "Here he was, just thinking out loud with his secretary. It was almost a personal sermon to me. Imagine what a great blessing it was for me to hear him compare one of his real-life experiences to his personal charge to lead the Church and its members."

Arthur's position and its demands were a way of life for the whole Haycock family. Whenever the president needed to go someplace, Arthur was there to take him. One summer morning, the Haycocks had their car packed for a vacation to Yellowstone National Park when the phone rang. The children begged their father not to answer, but he did. President Smith needed to go somewhere, and being at his side was Arthur's job. The car was unpacked, and the trip was postponed.

Children always captured the attention of President Smith. A widower for thirteen years, he almost adopted Arthur's daughters as his own, taking them to Saltair to ride the merry-go-round, to festivities and picnics. He invited the Haycock family to come to his house one afternoon and gave the girls a basket containing a beautiful white pedigreed Siamese kitten. They called it "Ming Toy." Not long after, Arthur received a hysterical call at the office. "Daddy, come home quick! Ming has bitten her tail and we can't catch her." Then came the second call, "We caught her." But Ming had left a trail. With her tail bleeding, she had scrambled around the furniture and brushed the walls with her tail. Everything she had touched looked as if it had been brushed with red paint.

President Smith kept a stack of children's books in his desk and various denominations of new silver coins in his pocket. Sometimes, if he ran out of new coins, he'd have Arthur use some mercury to polish some old ones. Every youngster who came to see him got a shiny piece of silver and a book. At Christmas, President Smith and Arthur visited the children at Primary Children's Hospital and presented each of them with a coin, a book, and, if they wanted one, a blessing.

In the cold winter season, President Smith usually spent

time in Southern California, and Arthur went with him. They stayed at a residence in Laguna Beach. One time Arthur left President Smith to rush home to check on his family. His wife, Maurine, had had a miscarriage and was flat in bed. Arthur was marooned in Milford, Utah, in a snowstorm. Finally he reached home, only to be called the next morning by President Smith with a plea to return quickly. He left that morning. Says Maurine, "They were difficult years, but we knew he was doing what the Lord intended for him, and he had our support."

When the Haycocks bought a new home in a subdivision developed for young families, President Smith insisted on visiting to "check things out." This was one of many instances when Arthur saw firsthand the practical interest of the Church leaders in the daily needs and circumstances of the Saints. President J. Reuben Clark came too, only to be dismayed that the home had no fireplace. "What are you going to do if the heat goes out?" President Clark queried. "How will you heat your home or cook your food if there's an electrical outage?"

President Smith's attention to other people was universal. He was a friend to everybody. Arthur recalls: "When I took President Smith home after work, he'd want to pick up those standing on street corners waiting for the bus. Sometimes I found myself miles from my home or his as I was dropping off the extra passengers."

One day President Smith and Arthur were looking out the window of the Smith home on Salt Lake City's east side when an old woman came by pulling a load of sticks. The prophet said to Arthur, "Look at that woman. Won't you get my car and take her home?" Arthur responded that he didn't know where she lived, she might not want to go home, she might not want to ride with him. But the president was firm: "You go and take her home. Remember, Arthur, she's somebody's mother."

President Smith suggested that Arthur take his car

because he had seen Arthur's car in action. A 1931 Pontiac with a leaky vinyl roof and four well-worn tires, it was less than dependable. Arthur would park the car about a block away from the president's home and then walk to the house so that the president wouldn't see it. One evening, faced with a flat tire and no spare in the trunk, he drove home on the rim rather than disturb the president. Arthur's car would start on its own—sometimes. Other times it had to be cranked. One night, however, Arthur was in a hurry and had parked near the president's house. After they had finished their business for the night, President Smith insisted on walking him to the car.

"Oh, you don't need to," said Arthur, but President Smith was determined. Arthur prayed that the car would start, and it did. Then it promptly died. He got out and had to crank it. Since the car did not have a gas throttle, he had to lift up the hood, put a stick between the carburetor and the foot feed, and then run around and pump the gas peddle, which would force the stick to fall out.

President Smith watched and paced, and Arthur got redder and redder. After two or three false starts, the engine finally caught hold. President Smith exclaimed, "I declare, I never saw a car started like that before!" "I declare" was one of his favorite phrases.

The president had a rubber mat under his office chair that would inch out on the nap of the carpet and up the wall with every movement. He'd say, "Arthur, what's the matter with this chair?" Arthur would give him a brief explanation about the nap of the rug and how every time he moved his chair the mat would slide and start creeping up the side of the wall. Every two or three days Arthur would have to pull the mat back into place, and President Smith would say, "Arthur, what's the matter with that thing?" Arthur would explain again about the nap and the movement of the chair, but that wasn't what President Smith wanted to hear. He'd just banter, "I declare, I declare, if it keeps this up we won't need that venetian blind."

Though a fastidious dresser, President Smith was not one for show. Once when he and Arthur passed a particularly well-dressed gentleman on the street, Arthur asked, "President, did you ever think of putting a hankie in your pocket like that?" He answered, "Yes, I thought about it once."

President Smith relied on his counselors and valued their expertise. Whenever he received a letter or discourse of substance, he would say, "I wonder what Reuben thinks of this?" and he'd be up on his feet and heading to President Clark's office. Arthur would race to open the door before the president reached it. President Clark, hunched over his work, would look up, strike his hand on his desk, and exclaim, "President Smith, you don't come to me, I come to you. You are the president and I am the counselor. When you want me, you call me." The reminder was soon forgotten when President Smith had another question and would say, "I wonder what Reuben thinks of this?" Arthur would leap for the door.

The president's style was simple. For breakfast he always ate steamed wheat. He liked it with warm cream and a dish of prunes. Arthur usually had Shredded Wheat or Wheaties. The president would say to Arthur, "You might as well cut the end off the broom or gather the shavings off the carpenter's floor as eat that. Why don't you have some of mine?" Arthur did, once, and much to his chagrin, the more he chewed, the bigger the wheat grew until he nearly choked. Everywhere the two went, they took a jar of wheat. The size of the jar depended on how long they were going to be gone. If they were out to dinner with others, Arthur would tell the waiter, "We're having roast beef, and he's having boiled wheat."

For lunch President Smith would have a soft-boiled egg, milk, homemade bread, and bottled fruit. At night he'd have a bowl of bread and milk with white seedless grapes. For a real treat he loved a chocolate shake or malt with a raw egg mixed into it. Arthur would have his shake straight—without the egg.

President Smith had a fine wit and a great sense of humor. In August 1950 he sailed to Hawaii for the celebration of the centennial of the Hawaiian mission. In the party were his daughters Emily and Edith, Elder and Sister Henry D. Moyle, and Arthur and Maurine.

They sat at the captain's table. While the others dined on steak and eggs for breakfast, pork chops for lunch, and prime rib for dinner, President Smith ate his regular fare of steamed wheat, boiled eggs, bread, and milk. Looking over the dinner menu one evening, he saw "Roast Capon in Burgundy" and thought he'd try it, since he'd grown fond of chicken dishes while serving on his mission in the Southern States. Emily nudged him, saying, "Papa, you don't want that; it's been cooked in burgundy." President Smith replied, "I don't care if it's been cooked in Australia. I still want it."

When the group arrived in Hawaii, word came that George F. Richards, president of the Quorum of the Twelve, had died. Arthur expected President Smith to turn around and go home, but after a lengthy telephone call with President Clark and President McKay, he determined to complete his conference assignment in the Islands and have his counselors carry out the funeral arrangements at home. To honor Elder Richards, President Smith dedicated the sessions in Hawaii to him. They also received word that Frank Evans, the finance secretary to the First Presidency, had passed away.

After being away a month, President Smith and Arthur were barely off the train when President Smith said, "I want to go call on those two widows." Their first stop was to see Sister Evans at the Eagle Gate apartments, where the president extended his sympathy and love. Having worked many years with Frank Evans, President Smith had great respect for his service to the Lord. Arthur recalls, "Since the couple had no children, he knew she would be lonely, and he told her she would be in his prayers."

The Richards's apartment was on the eighth floor of the Belvedere apartments, less than a block away. Betsy Hollings Richards had met President Richards when he was presiding over the Salt Lake Temple and she was working as a typist in the temple annex. After expressing his love for her and her husband, President Smith asked what he could do to help. She explained that before she married President Richards, she had been working in the index bureau of the temple. "If you could help me get that job back," she said, "I could make it." President Smith promised to do what he could, and the next day he secured her a job in the temple.

"This was President Smith doing what he liked to do most, comforting those in need and helping others," says Arthur. "His feelings for those suffering were real. Instead of rushing to the office to check his mail or going home to rest after the strenuous trip, he was concerned about those sisters who were alone, and he went to be with them."

It wasn't just Church officials that caught his attention. President Smith regularly visited the County Old Folks Home to shake hands with the residents. When ready to leave, he'd often comment to Arthur as he looked at the lonely people, "Isn't it strange that one mother can take care of ten children but ten children can't take care of one mother?"

President Smith also participated at the annual Old Folks Day at Salt Lake City's Liberty Park. "He was right at home with them," says Arthur. "He was a lot like Jesus, always ministering to the downtrodden, the aged, the ill, or anyone who was in need."

With President Smith, people came first. After attending some meetings in Denver, he and Arthur were hurrying to catch an overnight train for Salt Lake City when a woman caught Arthur's arm just as he was getting into the car to go to the station. She said she needed to talk to President Smith, and Arthur replied that the president was tired. She pleaded that she would just take a minute. President Smith, hearing her request, went right over to shake her hand. Standing beside her were three small children. She pulled a camera from her purse, and Arthur snapped a few photographs of the young family with President Smith. A few days later, a copy of one of the snapshots came in the mail. It showed President Smith patting one of the children on the head. With the photo was a note from the mother: "I am sending you this picture because it is a graphic illustration of the man we believe you are. The reason we treasure it so is because, as busy as you are, in spite of the fact you were being hurried into your car and then to the waiting train, you still took time to shake the hand of each child. You are a prophet of God with time for everyone."

President Smith was as interested in youth as he was in the elderly. While in England as an apostle, he had become acquainted with Lord Baden-Powell, founder of the Boy Scout movement. President Smith, George Q. Morris and Oscar A. Kirkham were responsible for bringing the Boy Scout program to the Church. President Smith was proud of that association and served on the National Executive Board of the Boy Scouts. He loved to dress in full Scout regalia and often attended official functions to honor young men advancing in the Scouting program.

President Smith almost always spoke extemporaneously. On October 1, 1948, he bore his testimony to the Saints: "I know that God lives. I know that Jesus is the Christ. And I am thankful to know that we are all brothers and sisters. Thankful that he gives us all opportunities to so adjust our lives here that when mortality is complete and our work is done that we will go to dwell in his presence and enjoy the companionship of those we love forever." (*Church News*, October 6, 1948, p. 3-c.)

*President and Sister
Grant with President
George Albert Smith
in his Scout uniform*

He advised the other General Authorities to speak from the heart as well. Elder Matthew Cowley was known for his inspirational messages that often focused on the blessings he gave, how the blind were healed, how the Lord cared for his children. At one conference session, Elder Cowley read his talk. Right after the meeting, President Smith called him in and said, "Don't let me ever catch you doing that again! You and the Lord do this. Don't get up and read. You get up and let the Spirit guide you."

On May 28, 1950, President Smith, Arthur, and Elder John A. Widtsoe went to Whitingham, Vermont, to dedicate a statue of Brigham Young at the second Church president's birthplace. In that setting, President Smith said, "We pray that thy Spirit may remain here that those who come to read the inscription on the monument may realize that thou art

36

the Father of us all and that he whom we are gathered to honor was one of thy choice sons who was great enough to assume his responsibilities and carry a tremendous load during his long lifetime." (*Improvement Era*, September 1950, p. 694.)

He also dedicated the statue of Brigham Young that stands in the United States Capitol rotunda. The local Utah committee, appointed by the governor, had originally suggested that President Smith write out and read his speech and his dedicatory prayer. They told Arthur, "President Smith tends to go on and on, and we don't want Utah to be embarrassed." Arthur, angry, said he would present the request to the president. Before Arthur had finished repeating the request, President Smith said to tell them to get somebody else. "He knew, and I knew, and they soon knew no one else could dedicate the statue of Utah's premier pioneer and second president of the Church but the current president of the Church," Arthur explains. When Arthur reported President Smith's response, the committee backed off in a hurry. According to Arthur, "President Smith gave the most magnificent talk you have ever heard in your life. He didn't ramble; the Lord used him. He knew it and I knew it."

In his prayer at the ceremonies in Washington, D.C., on June 1, 1950, President Smith paid tribute to a nation founded on true principles: "We pray that this statue, representing as it does a great people and great principles, may be the means of encouraging others to think of thee and honor thee, our Father." (Ibid.)

The vice-president of the United States, Alben Barkley, and many other dignitaries attended the ceremony, and the United States Marine Band provided the music. President Smith and Arthur had visited with President Harry Truman earlier that day. President Truman had opened his desk drawer in the Oval Office and said, "Look, President Smith, I've got my Book of Mormon right here." Arthur wasn't sure whether that book of scripture was always so handy. He thought perhaps President Truman had a secretary who understood how to make visitors feel welcome.

Shortly after the end of World War II, President Smith spoke to those attending a large funeral in a little town near Tremonton, Utah, to pay tribute to the four Borgstrom brothers who had been killed within six months of each other while serving in different branches of the service. The family, military brass, state officials, and reporters from the national press, including *Life* magazine, filled the chapel. Tall, rugged General Mark Clark, commander of Ninth Army, based in San Francisco, presided. A separate honor guard accompanied each casket. "I thought they would never stop coming," says Arthur. "President Smith gave the most magnificent talk on the Church. He gave the parents comfort, and he had all those hardened army officers in tears."

President Smith spoke at many funerals. His message usually included this thought: "I mourn with you but also I congratulate you that you have had the companionship of this wonderful person all these years, and that it will continue through the eternities."

President Smith had a favorite phrase, "We are all our Father's children," which appears on his gravestone. He took a particular interest in the Lamanites and in the descendants of the Prophet Joseph Smith who were members of the Reorganized Church of Jesus Christ of Latter Day Saints. There was a great love between him and Israel Smith, president of the Reorganized Church. Whenever George Albert Smith went East, he stopped in Independence, Missouri, to see his distant relative. When George Albert died in April 1951, Israel attended the funeral in the Tabernacle.

On Monday, April 9, 1951, each of the quorums stood to sustain the new president of the Church. Arthur was seated between George Albert Smith, Jr., and cousin Israel. All three stood and voted for David O. McKay as the new president of the LDS Church. On the hotel elevator after the funeral, Israel turned to Arthur and said, "You know, I didn't deserve many of the kind things that were done for me by my cousin George A."

Many were quick to suggest that George Albert Smith was just wasting his time trying to work with the Reorganized Church. But, says Arthur, his response was always the same: "I'm an old man. In the normal course of events it won't be long till I go to the other side and see my cousin Joseph, and I want to be able to say that while I was in mortality, I did everything in my power to bring his own flesh and blood into the Church for which he gave his life, and I don't want to have to hang my head.

"And when I see Father Lehi, I want to say I did everything I could to bring his posterity into the Church. I don't want to hang my head because I didn't do all I could for him as well."

When he became president of the Church, one of George Albert Smith's first actions was to set up a plan to assist the Lamanites. His interest in their behalf took him to Washington, D.C., and to numerous reservations in Utah, Arizona, New Mexico, Mexico, Hawaii, and Tonga. He blessed those who were sick, taught the gospel, sat at celebrations with tribal leaders, and paid tribute to his Lamanite friends. He met with councils in Idaho and agencies in New York to better conditions, broaden opportunities, and draw more attention to these Saints.

President Smith asked one of the newest members of the Council of the Twelve, Spencer W. Kimball, to be responsible for the Church's programs for the Lamanites. And Elder Kimball did. He developed such a love for the Lamanites that the Sioux Indians inducted him into their tribe and gave him the Indian name "Washti ho wombli," meaning "Good Voice Eagle" or "One who flies through the air and carries a good message." President Kimball, when called as president

Elder Spencer W. Kimball,
President George
Albert Smith, and
D. Arthur Haycock

of the Church, asked Elder Boyd K. Packer to watch over the Lamanite people.

President Smith's sensitivity to the needs of people was especially important after the devastation of World War II. He sent Elder Ezra Taft Benson to Europe to administer supplies stockpiled by the Saints in the United States during the war. When he went to Washington for help in shipping the materials, President Truman agreed to provide a ship but couldn't imagine what the members could send, since the country had been on such meager rations during the war. President Smith said, "We've been saving the wheat, while you've been plowing it under. We've got our granaries and our storehouses full, and we just need a ship to get all we've set aside to our destitute members in Europe."

Once while on assignment to a conference in Southern Utah, President Smith and Arthur stayed at the home of a rancher who raised sheep and turkeys. Very successful in his enterprises, the rancher had little time for observing the Sabbath Day or attending church.

Still, when the two visitors came to breakfast in the morning, all the chairs had been turned out from the table in preparation for family prayer. The rancher's six-year-old boy took one look at the arrangement of chairs and started to giggle. He was obviously trying to figure out how he was going to reach the table from such a strange angle, and he kept trying to get his father's attention. But his father hushed him up as President Smith proceeded to kneel and pray. After the prayer, the little boy piped up, "Daddy, what was that man saying to that chair?"

President Smith led the Church six years. When he became too ill to go to the office, Arthur brought the work to him at home and stayed many evenings to keep him company. When the two men watched on television the 1950 October conference in the president's living room on Yale Avenue, President Smith, who had been an apostle since 1903, commented, "This is the first time I have ever seen the faces of the speakers at conference. I have always either been sitting down in those seats with the speakers up behind me, or I was sitting in the seats by the podium and the speakers were standing in front of me."

November 2, 1950, was one of the last times President Smith was able to leave his home. He was very patriotic, and Arthur took him to vote.

On February 4, 1951, while in LDS Hospital, President Smith, in the presence of his daughter Edith, dictated to Arthur the thoughts on his mind: "Last evening and last night were the hardest for me. I felt like perhaps my time had come. If it has, it's all right; if not I'd appreciate the continuing faith and prayers of the people. Tomorrow is the regular meeting in the temple, and I would like the Brethren to lay the matter before the Lord.

"George, Arthur, and Albert know where all my account books are and where all my papers are indicating what should be done with my finances. . . . I'd like in the disposing of my funds for those that are most in need not to be overlooked. . . . Arthur, I don't want you to leave until I've had a blessing. I feel perfectly quiet and at peace. I am willing to stay or willing to go, whatever the Lord says. There is a lot in the world to do, and we should all do our part."

Two hours later when President Clark came, President Smith continued: "I've had a bad day, and I don't seem to be making any gain. I've been so weak for several days, but I am grateful to be as well as I am. Tomorrow is the meeting in the temple; I want you to take a message to the Brethren. I've lived a long time, and I'm in the midst of difficulty without question, and I seem to be unable to gain my strength. It's been suggested that I go to some other part of the country to try and get my strength, but the headquarters of the Lord's work is here. . . . I have two counselors in charge so that if the president is sick they can carry on. If the president is sick, things will go forward anyhow.

"President Clark, I want you to know you have been so considerate and kind. I have a real affection for you. I have no desire except to help you carry on the Lord's work. . . . I don't think my girls have any idea how near I've been to the other side. I haven't felt like my work was done at all. When my work is done, I want to go. One of my regrets is that I have been unable to organize a library and dispose of it. . . . As long as I have the money, I want to pay my hospital expenses; I don't want the Church to do it."

Addressing his secretary, President Smith said: "Arthur, I want you to know that I have absolute confidence in your faith and integrity and in you as a member of the Church. My family feels for you as I do. The Lord bless you, and many thanks for your kindnesses." In response to his request, President Clark and Arthur then gave the president a blessing.

President Smith's fine sense of humor stayed with him to the last. Just a day or two before he died, Arthur stepped up to his bed and said, "President, you look a little weary. Would you like to lie on your other side? I'll help you turn over." President Smith looked up with a twinkle in his eye and said, "Arthur, as long as I'm telling the truth, I don't care which side I lie on."

President Smith's son, George Albert, Jr., had planned to visit his father on his birthday on April 4. Leaving Boston, where he was a university professor, he stopped in Chicago for a meeting and was going to catch the train for Salt Lake City. Early on the morning of April 4, it was clear that the president was going to live hours, not days. Arthur quickly located Albert and asked him to go straight to the airport. Arthur had arranged for the president's son to fly home on a Portland-bound plane that would make an unscheduled landing in Salt Lake City. President Smith was still conscious when his son arrived home. "It made all the effort worthwhile," Arthur recalls. "It was touching for President Smith and his son to have that time together."

President Smith passed away that day, on his eighty-first birthday. His family and Arthur were at his bedside.

CHAPTER FOUR

David O. McKay

Tall, charismatic, and eloquent in quoting the scriptures, Browning, Burns, or Shakespeare, President David O. McKay was a vibrant and independent leader of The Church of Jesus Christ of Latter-day Saints. Scottish in ancestry and yet comfortable with world leaders from the South Pacific to Switzerland, he made a great impact on people wherever he went. He had been prepared to lead the Church since his call as an apostle in 1906 at age thirty-two, and he was sustained as president in 1951 at age seventy-seven. His influence reached around the world as the Church entered a new international era.

Arthur remembers those days in April 1951 after the death of President George Albert Smith as the First Presidency was reorganized. David O. McKay called as counselors Elder Stephen L Richards, his longtime associate in the Quorum of the Twelve, and President J. Reuben Clark, his fellow counselor under Presidents Grant and Smith. He appointed President Richards as first counselor and President Clark,who had formerly been first counselor in the Presidency, as second counselor. Thus, he followed apostolic seniority, for President Richards had been ordained an apostle in 1917, while President Clark had been ordained in 1934.

Arthur describes the positioning of these counselors as "a stunning moment for church leadership." When President Clark stood at the solemn assembly to address the Saints, he explained, "In The Church of Jesus Christ of Latter-day Saints, one takes the place to which one is duly called, which place one neither seeks nor declines. I earnestly pray that I may be the beneficiary of your prayers, and that I may be able to do the things which I am supposed to do with an eye single to the glory of our Heavenly Father."

For Arthur, that declaration held great personal significance as well, for he was no longer secretary to the prophet and president of the Church. Instead, President McKay asked him to assist Joseph Anderson, who was secretary to the First Presidency. While President McKay began to lead the burgeoning Church organization with the help of his longtime secretary Clare Middlemiss, Arthur focused on transcribing Brother Anderson's dictation from wax cylinders. For Arthur it was a difficult transition, but he refers to it as an important learning experience. "No one has a hold on a position in this Church," he says. "We are all simply serving others."

In November 1952, Dwight D. Eisenhower was elected president of the United States, and he immediately nominated Elder Ezra Taft Benson as Secretary of Agriculture. President McKay gave his blessing to this patriotic service. In turn, Arthur was offered a post as an administrative assistant to Elder Benson, which eventually took him to Washington. Not sure if he should leave Church employment, Arthur sought advice from President McKay, who was forthright: "You go, Arthur. It is right for you, and I have approved it." In early 1953, Arthur moved to Washington while his family stayed in Salt Lake City to sell their home. When he reached the nation's capital, he found living expenses higher than he had expected. He managed to rent a small room with a bath down the hall. He cooked his meals on a hot plate.

For Arthur, life at the Department of Agriculture in Washington, D.C., was a sharp contrast to life at Church

*Maurine and
D. Arthur Haycock
in Washington, D.C.*

headquarters in Salt Lake City. "The activity was intense, but the people there showed little interest in righteousness," he explains. "They were much more committed to getting ahead at all costs." Secretary Benson had strong leadership skills and responded well to the pace, the pressure, the structure, and the formality. He represented the Church well, and the government profited from his experience not only around the country but around the world. Always forthright and trusting, Secretary Benson expected similar integrity from others. "He was often disappointed, but he was undaunted," Arthur says. "He recognized this appointment as an opportunity for significant contribution to his country."

Arthur served with Secretary Benson in Washington for eighteen months. In June 1954, he was called by President Richards to preside over the Hawaii Mission. Returning to Salt Lake City, he met with the First Presidency before leaving for the mission and was set apart by President Clark. There was no training program to prepare the new president to administer one of the forty-two missions in the Church. President Richards outlined instructions and expectations in a few brief thoughts while walking up the front steps of the Church Administration Building with Arthur: "Remember to get your reports in on time. Don't disparage your predecessor. Keep to your budget. Now, the Lord bless you, and we'll see you when you get back."

Arthur, Maurine, and their four daughters, Marilyn, Judith Ann, Lynette, and Cheryl, arrived in Honolulu June 5, 1954. Elder LeGrand Richards, who was touring the mission with retiring mission president Ernest Nelson, met the Haycocks at the boat dock.

The mission home, which had been a center for servicemen during World War II, was in total disrepair. For several years the Haycocks made the best of it, but when Elder Marion G. Romney visited, Arthur put his fist through one of the big timbers under the front porch to demonstrate the damage to the structure from termites. After President Romney returned to headquarters, he received authorization for the purchase of a new mission home. An ideal facility was located in Nuuanu Valley, but the asking price was steep. Ralph Woolley, a prominent businessman and stake president, negotiated the purchase of the two and half acres, with the house and a small cottage for half the price. The mission had a new home.

The Haycocks kept in close touch with their friends on the mainland and received encouragement and advice from Church leaders. President Clark told Arthur in a letter, "I understand you are doing a good job. But always be sure that you get as many converts as you do baptisms." When Maurine's mother died, the Haycocks couldn't come home for the funeral, so Elder Spencer W. Kimball spoke at her funeral on their behalf.

Hawaii was a regular stop for Church officials on their way to New Zealand, Tahiti, Australia, and Asia. As a result, the Haycocks had lots of visitors. When President and Sister McKay were scheduled to tour the six missions in the Pacific in 1955, Arthur encouraged them to stop in Hawaii at the end of their trip. Though Arthur had had extensive experience in President George Albert Smith's office and was comfortable with the visits from General Authorities, he was anxious that all go well on President McKay's visit.

Arthur chartered a plane to fly the visitors from island to island. Though used to regular rainstorms, the pilot hit a squall and had difficulty breaking through the torrents pouring down on Hilo airport. As the pilot flew up the coast trying to find a break in the weather, Arthur grew more and more anxious. Then he glanced across the aisle and saw President McKay sleeping soundly. Arthur says, "He wasn't a bit worried, and the scene reminded me of the passage in the Bible that inspired the song, 'Master, the Tempest is Raging.' The apostles were so alarmed, but the Lord simply said, 'Peace, be still.' President McKay reflected that peace, and that put me at ease."

President McKay was well received by the people. On Molokai, one of the smaller islands, school children had been dismissed from classes to greet the religious leader. The Saints at the leper colony, Kalaupapa, painted rocks with their greeting, "Aloha McKay," which was read from the sky since the plane could not land at the tiny airport. On Maui the local authorities were the first to greet the visitors, and on the island of Hawaii all the local politicians joined the Mormons for a luau. Everywhere the group went, there was an honor guard of Boy Scouts.

President David O. McKay with his wife, Emma Ray Riggs McKay

During the tour, President McKay dedicated the grounds for the Church College of Hawaii. At the official ceremonies, Arthur was scheduled to introduce Sister McKay to the Saints. He had fretted over just the right words, finally saying, "This is Sister Emma Rae Riggs McKay, who is just as lovely now as she was fifty-four years ago when President McKay married her." Suddenly Arthur felt President McKay's hand on his shoulder. Taking the microphone from Arthur, President McKay said, "I just want to correct Brother Haycock and say that my dear wife, Mama Rae, is fifty-four years lovelier than she was when I married her." When President McKay asked the advisory committee when they planned to open the school, he was told it would be in eighteen months, in the fall of 1956. The prophet responded, "No, I want it to open this year, the fall of 1955." The committee set to work purchasing five war-surplus barracks from Pearl Harbor to be used as classrooms, offices, and a library, and on September 26, 1955, the college opened.

The completed college facilities were dedicated December 17, 1958. At that time President McKay said, "From this school will go men and women whose influence will be felt for good towards the establishment of peace internationally. Nearly a billion people are waiting to hear our message over in China. I don't know how many millions in Japan, 350 million in India. We have scarcely touched these great nations, and they are calling today, as the people's voice in Macedonia called to the Apostle Paul, 'Come over and help us!' "

On February 10, 1955, President McKay held an informal meeting for forty-four members at Pulehu, Maui, the site of the first baptisms on Hawaii and the location of the first branch of the Church in the Hawaiian islands, organized August 6, 1851. President McKay related to the assembled Saints a spiritual experience he and Brother Hugh J. Cannon had shared in 1921 at that spot while on a world tour of Church missions.

As background he explained that Hugh J. Cannon's father, George Q. Cannon, was one of the first missionaries to serve in Hawaii and had converted many of the islanders, including the influential Judge Jonatana H. Napela. Eventually he and other natives helped Elder Cannon translate the Book of Mormon into Hawaiian. Elder Cannon and the islanders had built a Church meetinghouse at the location where the visitors now stood.

President McKay, standing on the location of a pepper tree that had recently blown down in a storm, recounted his visit thirty-four years earlier, explaining: "We became very much impressed with the surroundings, . . . so I said, 'I think we should have a word of prayer.' It was a hot day, and the sun was shining, so we retired to the shade of a pepper tree. . . .

I offered the prayer. We all had our eyes closed, and it was a very inspirational gathering. As we started to walk away at the conclusion of the prayer, Brother Keola Kailimai took Brother E. Wesley Smith [the mission president and son of Joseph F. Smith] to the side and very earnestly began talking to him in Hawaiian. . . . Brother . . . Smith said, 'Brother McKay, . . . Brother Kailimai said that while you were praying, and we all had our eyes closed, he saw two men who he thought were Hugh J. Cannon and E. Wesley Smith step out of line in front of us and shake hands with someone, and he wondered why Brother Cannon and Brother Smith were shaking hands while we were praying. He opened his eyes, and there stood those two men still in line, with their eyes closed just as they had been. He quickly closed his eyes because he knew he had seen a vision.'

"Now Brother Hugh J. Cannon greatly resembled Brother George Q. Cannon, his father. E. Wesley Smith has the Smith attribute just as President [Joseph F. Smith had it.] Naturally, Brother Keola Kailimai would think that these two men were there. I said, 'I think it was George Q. Cannon and Joseph F. Smith, two former missionaries to Hawaii, whom that spiritual-minded man saw.'

"We walked a few steps farther, and I said, 'Brother Kailimai, I do not understand the significance of your vision, but I do know that the veil between us and those former missionaries was very thin.' Brother Hugh J. Cannon who was by my side, with tears rolling down his cheeks, said, *'Brother McKay, there was no veil.'* "

Concluding, President McKay said, "The Lord is pleased with what the missionaries have done, and I am grateful for the response of the Hawaiian people and others of these lovely islands. . . . May we who will now have increased responsibility from this moment on be true to the trust that the Lord has in us!" (*Cherished Experiences,* compiled by Clare Middlemiss [Salt Lake City: Deseret Book Co., 1955], pp. 50–52.)

Arthur had seen President McKay perform miracles in Hawaii when they visited in 1937. Serving on the big island of Hawaii, Arthur and his companion were checking daily on the progress of one of the missionaries who was in a

*D. Arthur Haycock, his wife, Maurine, and their four daughters
on their way home from Hawaii*

small country hospital with typhoid fever. The elder was delirious most of the time, and the two young missionaries were discouraged. President McKay was touring the Hawaiian mission, visiting Hilo at the other end of the island, when he heard of the elder's plight. He traveled three hundred miles to reach the rural hospital and invited Arthur and his companion to join him in laying on hands and giving the patient a blessing. "There was a sweet, comforting spirit in the room as President McKay pleaded with the Lord for the health of our companion," Arthur says. "He promised him a full recovery." It wasn't long before the elder was back at work in the mission. "This remarkable healing was a great inspiration and testimony builder to all the missionaries," says Arthur. "President McKay did not hesitate to make the long journey to seek out one sick missionary and bless him with full health."

In July 1958 the Haycocks were released after having

presided over the mission for four years. Arthur had employment offers from a variety of hotel chains, public relations firms, and health organizations in Hawaii and Los Angeles, but he felt impressed to return to Salt Lake City. Since his first job at the Church, he had always done what the authorities had asked him to do. He hoped to go back to work for the Church, telling his friends, "Think of the company I'll keep."

Elder Mark E. Petersen, the last official visitor to the mission before Arthur's release, spoke plainly: "Don't take anything until you hear from me." As president of Deseret News Publishing Company, Elder Petersen asked Arthur to become the secretary-treasurer of that corporation. Arthur started work August 3, 1958.

Four years later Elder Spencer W. Kimball asked Arthur to meet with the executive committee of the Missionary Committee, which, besides Elder Kimball, included Elders Gordon B. Hinckley and Boyd K. Packer. They asked Arthur to become the executive secretary of the Missionary Committee. He accepted and moved back to the fourth-floor offices of the Missionary Department in the Church Administration Building.

Arthur enjoyed the job. He knew missionary work from the field, and from Church headquarters as well. His understanding of the entire Church operation had increased.

It was not surprising, therefore, that at ten minutes to eight one Thursday morning, he received a summons from Elder Harold B. Lee, who was calling at the direction of the Quorum of the Twelve Apostles. Arthur was to bring a shorthand book and come at once to the temple. He was appointed the new secretary to the Council of the Twelve.

President McKay's health had been failing. On Sunday, January 18, 1970, Arthur was sitting in a stake high council meeting when word came that President McKay had died.

When he heard the news, Arthur went directly to President McKay's apartment in the Hotel Utah. Joseph Fielding

Smith, president of the Quorum of the Twelve, and Harold B. Lee, who would become the next president of that quorum, had just arrived and were talking with the family. Arthur joined them in contacting the members of the Twelve who were away on assignments and arranging for their prompt return.

A grand era in the Church had ended. For nineteen years this stately, gracious Church president had guided the growth of the Church around the world, prompting people to love one another and stay close to their families. Though Arthur was not as close to President McKay as he had been to President George Albert Smith, he affirms, "I had a testimony of his calling and his responsibility and valued my role in sustaining him as the president of the Church. Like members of the Church everywhere, I prayed for President McKay. I loved him.

"During his tenure I saw the Church from many vantages—the mission field, the government, the press, and the highest councils." It was these experiences that prepared Arthur to help other Church presidents in years to come.

President McKay trained many of the present General Authorities. He called President Gordon B. Hinckley as an Assistant to the Council of the Twelve in 1958 and as an apostle in 1961. When the Church decided to build a temple in Switzerland, new challenges arose. The Swiss temple was to serve Saints all over Europe. How would the temple handle all the different languages? How would such a small country staff a temple for such a large area? President McKay gave the assignment to Elder Hinckley to put the endowment ceremony on film.

It was a first for the Church. Elder Hinckley selected the actors and directed the filming, with the dubbing in of translations in many languages. Later, as temples were dedicated in other parts of the world, the endowment was translated into additional languages.

"All that training under President McKay and subsequent presidents prepared President Hinckley for his challenges during President Spencer W. Kimball's administration. President Kimball was sick in his later years, and Brother Hinckley had to carry so much of the day-to-day burden," Arthur says. President Hinckley as a counselor to President Kimball dedicated sixteen temples in countries around the world, including Tonga, Chile, Sweden, South Africa, and Australia. As a counselor to President Benson, he has dedicated another eight in such areas as Peru, Canada, and Nevada.

"President McKay was a great man, a good man, who accomplished much in the nineteen years he served as prophet, seer, and revelator," according to Arthur. Arthur learned early in working at the Church offices that there would always be individual styles of leadership but that the principles that sustained the work would be inviolate. "President McKay exercised a scholarly, academic style," he says, "but he was also a courageous leader with strong opinions that could be easily measured." It was President McKay who challenged the Church membership with the slogan "Every member a missionary."

The Lord gave President McKay a sense of vision and an understanding of the worldwide Church. He was the most widely traveled of any Church president to that time. Everywhere he went he encouraged the members to focus on gospel principles in the home. His testimony of personal application of the gospel was one of his favorite themes: "Only through individual effort and divine guidance may true success and happiness be obtained. There is no blessing based upon another's achievement. Everyone must work out his own salvation." (*Cherished Experiences,* pp. 9–10.)

CHAPTER FIVE

Joseph Fielding Smith

President Joseph Fielding Smith is described by Arthur Haycock as the "Rock of Gibraltar." Called as an apostle in 1910 at age thirty-three, he was sustained as president of the Church on January 23, 1970, at age age ninety-three. No other Church president began his tenure at such an advanced age.

"Joseph Fielding Smith came to earth with a mission," Arthur contends. Arthur was serving as the secretary to the Council of the Twelve Apostles when President Smith was named tenth president of the Church, the sixth prophet in this century. "You knew if you walked in his footsteps, you would not deviate from the gospel." He asked Arthur to be his secretary, and they began to develop a close and unusual bond. Arthur says: "His manner appeared strict and exacting, yet he was tender and warm. He was driven to preach the gospel, to tell the world, 'There is one Lord, one faith, one baptism, one God and Father of us all, and one true church, the only true and living church upon the face of the whole earth.' He was indeed prepared to lead the Church."

President Smith's command of the scriptures was without equal; his understanding of the development of the Church was a product of his forty-five years of service as Church Historian. His decades of experience in Church administration—sixty years as an apostle—exceeded that of any other General Authority. "He came to the position an elderly man," says Arthur, "but a wise one who had influenced the Church's growth from its Rocky Mountain roots to its position as a religious force in the world today."

When President Smith died on July 2, 1972, at age ninety-five, the Church lost its living link to the pioneer past. Known for his historical roots in the Church and for his books on doctrinal subjects, President Smith was the son of the sixth president of the Church, Joseph F. Smith, and the grandson of the Patriarch Hyrum Smith, who was martyred in Carthage Jail. He was the grandnephew of the Prophet Joseph Smith. Because of these roots, President Smith held great reverence for the Church, its priesthood, and its responsibilities in the latter days.

When President Smith moved from the Historian's office to the president's office on the main floor of the Church Administration Building, he intended to use another desk rather than the one that was there—until Arthur showed him that the desk had been used by his father. President Joseph F. Smith had signed his name on a desk drawer with the date April 5, 1913, which prompted President Smith to change his mind. The desk was also used later by Presidents Harold B. Lee and Spencer W. Kimball.

President Smith also had a close affinity for the temple. At the Ogden Temple dedication, January 18, 1972, he looked back at the dedication of the Salt Lake Temple in April 1893. He had been one of those attending those significant services and had served in the Salt Lake Temple presidency from 1915 to 1935. As he spoke at the Ogden services, he challenged the members: "May I remind you that when we dedicate a house to the Lord, what we really do is dedicate ourselves to the Lord's service." (*Church News*, January 22, 1972, p. 3.)

Three weeks later, on February 9, 1972, he presided over the dedication of the Provo Temple, an occasion Arthur remembers as a glorious event for President Smith, whose dedicatory prayer paid special tribute to his grandfather:

"Today is the 172nd [birthday] . . . of my grandfather, the Patriarch Hyrum Smith, and I am pleased that we are celebrating that occasion by presenting to the Lord another holy temple, wherein those keys and powers, held jointly by him and the Prophet Joseph Smith, may be used for the salvation and exaltation of many of our Father's children." (Ibid., February 12, 1972, p. 3.)

President Smith had a tremendous love for his own father. He often used to say to Arthur, "My father never had time to be a boy." Joseph F. Smith had driven an ox team across the plains with his mother when he was just a boy, and at age fifteen, orphaned, he was sent on a mission to Hawaii, where he served four and a half years. Since Arthur had been a missionary and mission president in Hawaii, the two spent many hours discussing the islands where President Smith's father had spent so much time. They also visited Hawaii together in 1972.

President Smith enjoyed recounting stories of his childhood. Arthur remembers one in particular about a pony. President Smith grew up in Salt Lake City not far from the Church offices. Behind the Smith home was a barn, where young Joseph Fielding kept his pet pony, Junie. Out in the yard was a watering trough for the cow and the pony. The yard was surrounded by a high fence with a gate secured by a piece of wood that slid into a slot. If Junie got thirsty in the middle of the night, she'd slip the bar up with her nose and wander out to the trough in the yard to get a drink. She learned to turn the tap on with her teeth, but she never turned it off. By morning, the trough would be spilling over into the yard, wasting precious water and forming a massive mud puddle.

Joseph's father, then president of the Church, became impatient with the situation, and one day he said, "Joseph, why don't you take care of that horse? We can't afford to have this yard a swamp all the time."

Joseph replied that he did take care of the horse. Not satisfied with the answer, his father said, "You come with me and I'll show you how to take care of the problem." Using a leather strap from the barn, he carefully wrapped it around the gate and secured it with a buckle. Then he said, "See, that was easy. That takes care of it, and we won't have this problem again." Looking at his young son he added, "I can't understand why you didn't think of it."

By the time the two got about halfway across the yard, the pony was right on their heels, nudging them along with her nose. Not only could she turn on the tap but she could unbuckle a strap as well.

Arthur was introduced to President Smith's humor when he was assigned to the Finance Department in his first years in Church employment. After lunch at the Lion House one day, Arthur saw someone go up the back stairs into the Church Administration Building next door. Arthur thought that if he hurried, he could get into the building without having to search his pockets for the key. He darted up the steps and caught the door just before it closed. As he rushed into the elevator, the only one to service the building, he found he had been following Elder Smith. Young and inexperienced, Arthur tried to make conversation with the apostle, blurting out, "I just followed you in the back door and caught the elevator door before it closed. I'm kind of hoping that's how it will be on the other side. If I can catch the pearly gates before they close behind someone like you, I may make it."

Elder Smith looked Arthur up and down. Then, as the elevator doors slid open, he winked and said, "If I were you, my brother, I wouldn't count on it."

Though quiet and soft-spoken, President Smith was deliberate and definite in his ways, says Arthur, who learned of those traits while he was secretary to the Council of the Twelve. One day Arthur was sorting out a mass of papers across the table in a room where the Twelve often met for meetings. President Smith didn't approve of his usurping

*President Joseph
Fielding Smith with
a young admirer*

the room for his secretarial needs and reminded him of the sacred purpose of the room. Arthur moved his materials elsewhere.

Arthur remembers when the president of the Church could go almost anywhere in the world with little fanfare. Gradually it became necessary to tighten security around the Brethren. Before that time, the General Authorities would leave general conference through the back door of the Tabernacle, where a passage would be roped off to provide a path for them to the street and their cars. This allowed them to leave Temple Square more quickly, but not everyone observed the restrictions. Once a little girl slipped under the ropes and came up to President Smith's side. He leaned down, picked her up, and gave her a gentle hug. It was a scene Arthur will never forget. "That little girl nestled next to his cheek as if he were her grandfather," he recalls. "The way he smiled and hugged her close reflected all his love and devotion for the Saints." Later the little girl's parents scolded her for getting lost in the crowd. She said, "I wasn't lost. I was in the arms of the prophet."

President Smith never veered from his course; people always knew where he stood. "He wasn't flashy," Arthur explains. "He never made anyone laugh in conference. I can't ever remember him telling a joke at the pulpit. His was always a solemn gospel dissertation that was a result of his intense family tradition of faith and service. He had something to say to the Saints, and it was always serious." His opening sermon at general conference on October 1, 1971, was typical of his counsel: "We believe that worship is far more than prayer and preaching and gospel performance. The supreme act of worship is to keep the commandments, to follow in the footsteps of the Son of God, to do ever those things that please him. It is one thing to give lip service to the Lord; it is quite another to respect and honor his will by following the example he has set for us." (*Conference Report*, October 1971, p. 6.)

While to some President Smith appeared rigid and autocratic because of his sober sermons, close associates described him as "a true friend, gentle, kind, shy, and tender." Arthur characterizes him as reserved, but this quality came from shyness and humility. "In spite of his great wisdom and mastery of the scriptures, he was a simple man with simple faith. He had only one purpose in life, and that was to serve the Lord and his Church," Arthur says.

President Smith's wife, Jessie Evans Smith, was in many ways his opposite. She was outgoing, gregarious, and affable. Arthur claims that they made an unusual couple. Joseph Fielding Smith had been in her home as a ward teacher, and the two renewed their acquaintance when she called him from the County Clerk's office to arrange an appointment at the Church Historian's office to have him sign a document. Gentleman that he was, President Smith said he would come to her office. He had been married twice before to Louie Shurtliff and Ethel Georgina Reynolds, both of whom had

61

died. When Joseph and Jessie were married in the Salt Lake Temple, President Grant said at the conclusion of the ceremony, "Now, Joseph, kiss your wife." President Smith referred to that directive in an interview on their thirty-third wedding anniversary, April 12, 1971, commenting, "He said it like he meant it, and I have been doing it ever since."

President and Sister Smith were unusually devoted to each other. Arthur still pictures them walking together and chatting. The president usually carried her purse, a satchel full of everything she might need. When she urged the president to rest, Arthur recalls, she'd say, "Now, lie down and take a nap after church. All the other presidents did." He would quip, "Well, where are they now?"

When the two visited wards or stakes, they would usually end up singing. Jessie had a beautiful voice. A former member of the Mormon Tabernacle Choir, she would accompany their singing on the piano. President Smith would turn to the audience and say, "She calls this a duet; I call it a Do-It. I have to Do-It whether I want to or not." Even in President Smith's later years, they loved to sing for the Saints. At the conclusion of their musical number, President Smith would often turn to the audience and say, "I appreciate that you folks didn't walk out on me."

Driving back to Salt Lake City after an impromptu recital at a Brigham Young University devotional, Arthur turned to the president and said, "President Smith, those people loved you, and they enjoyed your singing. Did you see they were weeping during your duet?" President Smith quickly replied, "I can understand that. My singing is enough to make anybody cry."

President Smith had great reverence for nature. No matter where he went in the world, he took time to view the scenery—the ocean, the mountains, the plains, the birds, the clouds, the flowers. As Arthur recalls, "He would find a sermon in simple things that we often overlook. He marveled at the magnificence of the world around us."

President Joseph Fielding Smith and his wife, Jessie Evans Smith, singing a "Do-It" at the piano

President Smith enjoyed fresh fruit, especially watermelon and strawberries. He and Sister Smith enjoyed snacking on fruit. When they traveled, they sometimes stopped at a roadside stand to buy strawberries, which they would eat right out of the cup. President Smith also had two favorite kinds of pie—hot and cold. Like his historical research or his study of the scriptures, he was methodical about the way he ate pie: first he would cut off and eat the crust, then he'd polish off the rest.

President Smith's words touched the hearts of people everywhere. When the BYU student body awarded him the Exemplary Manhood Award, he urged the young people to follow the counsel of the Apostle James: "Take, my brethren, the prophets, who have spoken in the name of the Lord, for an example." (James 5:10.) President Smith added, "The greatest example set for men, was that of [Jesus Christ]. His

*President
Joseph Fielding Smith
and D. Arthur Haycock*

life was perfect. He did all things well and was able to say to all men, 'follow thou me' and we should all pattern our lives after His." (*Church News*, April 22, 1972, p. 3.)

In April 1971, President Smith addressed 13,000 young people in Long Beach, California, saying, "I plead with you young people . . . to keep yourselves clean and pure so that you will be entitled to go to the house of the Lord and together with the companions of your choice, enjoy all [the] greatest blessings the Lord offers to you." (Ibid., April 24, 1971, p. 6.)

President Smith's life was totally devoted to the Lord, and he always felt comfortable talking about the Savior and the gospel plan. To Arthur, the breakfast table seemed an unlikely place for a gospel dissertation, but not to President Smith. One day at breakfast he told Arthur, "I can't wait to get over to the other side and thank Mother Eve for what she did. We wouldn't be here if it weren't for her. Then I think of the Savior born in a manger. I think of him sweating drops of blood and hanging on the cross." President Smith was not one who often shed tears in public, but on this occasion the tears were streaming down his face as he said, "You know, he did that for me. He did that for us all. How can we ever repay him for his redeeming sacrifice?"

"President Smith's testimony was not melodramatic or complex," Arthur explains. "It was simple, sincere, and from the heart. It was clearly given to guide us all."

In July 1970, when Sister Smith was hospitalized for several weeks, President Smith stayed in her hospital room at night, sleeping on a couch near her bed until she could go home.

The following summer he was making plans with Arthur for the Church's first area conference, to be held in Manchester, England, when Sister Smith became ill. Arthur, who had been spending much of his time with them at their home in the Eagle Gate apartments, took her and President Smith to the hospital. She was diagnosed with congestive heart failure and was hospitalized immediately. She stayed almost a month and, as before, President Smith stayed at her side. When she was able to leave, they moved into the eighth-floor suite at the Hotel Utah where President and Sister McKay had lived.

On August 3 Sister Smith was checked by the doctor to see if she would be able to make the trip abroad to the area conference. At eight that evening, her nurse called Arthur, who was working late at the Church offices, and said to come quickly. As soon as he arrived, Arthur could see that Sister Smith was dying. Knowing that several of the General Authorities were attending a dinner at the Lion House, he hurried up the street and found Elder Richard L. Evans and President Harold B. Lee. By the time the three arrived at the hotel, Sister Smith had died. As they gathered around President Smith to express their love, he said simply, "I have been through this three times now."

Sister Smith's funeral was held in the Tabernacle. In benediction to her long life, the Tabernacle Choir, with whom she had sung for more than forty years, sang "King of Glory," from which comes the song she had sung so often, "He that Hath Clean Hands and a Pure Heart."

A week later President Smith and Arthur left for the conference meetings in Manchester, England. "It was a difficult period," says Arthur. "President Smith was heartsick and lonely; he struggled with Jessie's loss."

President Smith was used to having his wife at his side when he spoke. He had his sermons typed on yellow sheets, which he folded in half and put in his left coat pocket. Just before he gave a sermon she would jokingly remind him, "Your *palk* is in your *tocket*." The two would then chuckle, and he would get up and take out his talk and read it. In England she wasn't there to give him that support. Still, his message to the Saints came through clearly. Speaking five times during the conference, President Smith said, "We are members of a world church, a church that has the plan of life and salvation, a church set up by the Lord himself in these last days to carry his message of salvation to all his children in all the earth. . . . Not only shall we preach the gospel in every nation before the second coming of the Son of Man, but we shall make converts and establish congregations of Saints among them." (*Manchester Area Conference Report*, August 1971, p. 5.)

When not in meetings, the conference visitors took in some of the sights at Cardiff, Wales. While others in his party were visiting a splendid castle, President Smith, worn out from traveling, was not even interested in getting out of the car. Donald Smith, his nephew and doctor who was in the party, coaxed, "Uncle Joseph, don't you want to go home and say you have set foot on Wales?" President Smith opened the car door and set one foot firmly on the pavement. "There!" he announced. "I have set foot on Wales." Then he climbed back into the car and shut the door.

While President Smith was in England, his daughter Amelia and her husband, Bruce R. McConkie, a member of the Council of the Twelve, moved all of the president's personal things to their home, where he lived until his death.

Arthur usually picked up President Smith in the morning and took him home after work. President Smith had always adhered to the counsel in the Doctrine and Covenants, "Retire to thy bed early, that ye may not be weary; arise early, that your bodies and your minds may be invigorated." (D&C 88:124.) All his life he was up by six in the morning and in his office by eight. As president he continued this regimen. In the last week before his death, he worked in his office, signed papers, met with his counselors, and posed with the switchboard operators for a photograph. He even visited the Historical Department to see former fellow workers.

President Smith gave his last official address at the mission president's seminar on June 29, 1972. "His words were a fitting conclusion to a life devoted to the Lord," Arthur says. In his remarks he wished the leaders "success . . . as you walk humbly before Him. . . . You have been called to serve in the most important work in the world. It was the Prophet Joseph Smith himself who said: 'After all that has been said, the greatest and most important duty is to preach the gospel.' " (*Church News,* July 8, 1972, p. 5.)

Elder Ezra Taft Benson spoke at that same seminar, and his message was timely: "The saving of the souls of men is the greatest work that is going on in the whole universe. It is going on both sides of the veil; and I think sometimes that it doesn't matter which side of the veil we are working on."

On July 2, 1972, Elder Bruce R. McConkie called Arthur and said, with urgency in his voice, "Pick up the president's daughter Josephine [who lived in Bountiful], and come quick." Arthur asked, "Is something wrong?" Elder McConkie replied quickly, "Yes. Hurry!"

When Arthur and Josephine arrived at the McConkie home, President Smith was lying on the couch in the living room. He had just passed away. He had been sitting in his chair looking out the window when, without struggle or pain, he had slipped peacefully away. He was ninety-five; he would have turned ninety-six later that month.

Following the funeral services in the Tabernacle, the Twelve Apostles met in the temple July 7, 1972, to reorganize the First Presidency. Arthur was invited to attend and recalls the experience: "Each one of the Council of the Twelve expressed himself.They were sitting in their usual places, with no one sitting in the First Presidency chairs. The youngest member of the Twelve spoke first and bore his testimony and said he felt that the Presidency should be reorganized at once, and then each of the members of the Twelve in turn continued on in the same manner, expressing themselves, until it was President Kimball's turn. He, too, expressed his feelings that the First Presidency should be reorganized at once, and as the senior member under President Lee, he claimed the privilege of nominating Harold B. Lee as president of the Church. The voting was unanimous, and President Kimball was voice in ordaining and setting President Lee apart.

"President Lee then took his place in the center chair of the three for the First Presidency in the upper room of the temple. He named President N. Eldon Tanner as his first counselor and President Marion G. Romney as his second. These brethren were then set apart for these positions."

CHAPTER SIX

Harold B. Lee

On October 6, 1972, during general conference, Harold B. Lee was sustained as the eleventh president of The Church of Jesus Christ of Latter-day Saints. In his address he said, "Today is the greatest moment of my life. There has been here an overwhelming spiritual endowment, attesting no doubt, that in all likelihood we are in the presence of personages, seen and unseen, who are in attendance. Who knows but that even our Lord and Master would be near us on such an occasion as this, for we, and the world must never forget that this is his church, and under his almighty direction we are to serve."

Though President Lee was a man of great abilities and accomplishments, he humbly acknowledged that he was simply on the Lord's errand. He told seventy-five press representatives at a news conference that he felt very much like Nephi when he said, "I, Nephi, . . . went forth . . . , not knowing beforehand the things which I should do." (See 1 Nephi 4:5–6.) When asked about the greatest challenge facing the Church leaders, President Lee replied, "Keeping pace with the growth of the membership." At every opportunity he counseled the Saints, "The safety of the Church lies in the members keeping the commandments. There is nothing more important that I could say. Keep the commandments and blessings will come."

This was a man who was inspiring and fearless. Arthur

Haycock, who served as President Lee's secretary, observes, "He was in control at all times, saying what needed to be said and doing what needed to be done. But you always knew that he would then report to the Lord.

"He was deeply spiritual. He was so close to the other side that he often said that there was no veil. For him, I know that was true. He did not wear his sensitivity on his sleeve. He was always in tune with the Spirit, but he was always in touch with the people as well. He had a remarkable gift as a leader."

President Lee exemplified such meekness when he spoke to the youth at a fireside in the Salt Lake Tabernacle on August 19, 1972. It was one of his first major speeches as Church president. He said, "Pray for me, young people. I plead with you to pray for me, and I promise you that I will try to so live, that the Lord can answer your prayers through me."

Having served in many ecclesiastical positions, President Lee was well prepared for his assignment. He was a seminary teacher at South High School in the school's first year of operation, and Arthur was one of his students. "With his dark wavy hair he was dramatic in his appearance," Arthur recalls, "but what I remember most was the way he took his work and the gospel so seriously. We knew it was important to him."

Arthur also remembers the day he was saying the opening prayer in seminary when he felt himself swaying back and forth. He opened his eyes to see what was happening, and the students were all holding on to their desks, their faces drained of color. It was an earthquake, and Brother Lee rushed them all outside to safety. Arthur never finished that prayer.

Neither President Lee nor Arthur could have imagined the way their lives would weave together. President Lee, as a member of the Council of the Twelve, ordained Arthur to be a bishop in 1947, and the two later worked together at

*President Harold B. Lee
and President
Spencer W. Kimball
exchanging greetings*

Church headquarters. Arthur served as secretary to the Council of the Twelve when President Lee was an apostle and eventually as his secretary when President Lee directed the whole Church.

"President Lee was wise. You knew his suggestions were thoughtful, sensible, and inspired," says Arthur. "He could speak on behalf of the Church or he could address the needs of just one person." When Arthur was working as secretary and treasurer at the *Deseret News* after he presided over the Hawaii Mission, he was approached by Elders Spencer W. Kimball, Gordon B. Hinckley, and Boyd K. Packer to take a position in the Missionary Department under their direction. He pondered whether to accept the post and finally went to Elder Lee for advice. Elder Lee responded, "The

71

offer may not be coming to you by inspiration, but if Spencer W. Kimball is asking you to do it, it's the closest thing to it. He is the biggest short man that I know anywhere. Anything Spencer W. Kimball wants, I'd listen."

President Lee was a leader who appealed to young and old alike. He often cautioned the youth, "I have the responsibility to speak by the Spirit of the Lord, and you have the responsibility to listen by the Spirit of the Lord." (*Church News*, June 16, 1973, p. 3.)

At Ricks College President Lee gave one of the finest speeches Arthur ever heard. He counseled the students who were witnessing dissension on college campuses across the nation to have faith in America, declaring, "Men may fail in this country, earthquakes may come, seas may heave themselves beyond their bounds, there may be great drought and hardship as we may call it, but this nation, founded on principles laid down by men whom God raised up, will never fail. This is the cradle of humanity where life on this earth began in the Garden of Eden. This is the place where the new Jerusalem is; this is the place which the Lord said is favored above all the nations in the world. This is the place where the Savior will come to his temple. I have faith in America. You and I must have faith in America if we understand the teachings of the gospel of Jesus Christ."

The students showed their admiration for this great leader with the following tribute presented during his visit: "As sons and daughters of the living God, we stand united in tribute to the living prophet. . . . Called from the simplicity of farms and fields to stand in the upper rooms of the temple where the veil is thinnest, comes such a man, whose life is a testimony that speaks to the praises of God. This is a man who is more than a man, a man bearing Israel's prophetic inheritance, one of God's choicest sons."

Not long after President Lee was sustained as the president of the Church, he received a note from a Primary president with a touching story: "I held up your picture and said to the children that this was our new president of the Church, Harold B. Lee. A little hand shot up quickly. 'Oh, I know him,' said the little boy. 'We sing about him all the time in church: Reverent-lee, quiet-lee . . . ' "

Arthur describes President Lee as always dressed in neatly pressed suits and carefully knotted ties. "He looked impeccable and stood with such imposing stature. You seldom spoke lightly or facetiously around him. He set a formal tone in his meetings, yet no one was more gracious or more considerate. He was formal in his relationships," says Arthur.

Once in a stake conference talk Arthur apologized for his height. He had been five foot six since high school, and he explained that he had tried lifts in his shoes, but he never got any taller. President Lee spoke right after Arthur and scolded him in front of the congregation, saying, "I never want to hear you talk like that again. I measure people from the shoulders up."

President Lee was a forceful and able administrator. One of the hallmarks of his style was that he cared deeply about people and took time for them. His service as president was marked by announcements of new missions and major building projects. President Lee pushed himself to the limit. When he was in Mexico in 1972, he spoke to four different groups in one night. "He was driven to do all he could as fast as he could," says Arthur. But he, like those before him and after him, always took time to help with individual needs. He once said of a spiritual experience, "It seemed as though the heavens opened and I could encompass every member of the church and my love went out to every member of the church and in fact to the whole world." He called people on the phone who sent him letters and talked with them about their problems and concerns. He cared deeply about needs and expectations and issues facing the people universally and individually.

The Haycocks often traveled with the Lees. Their most

President Harold B. Lee and his wife, Freda Joan Jensen Lee,
with Brother and Sister Haycock

unusual trip was when they joined Elder Lee and his new
bride Freda Joan Jensen Lee after their honeymoon in
Hawaii in 1963. At the time, Arthur was secretary to the
Quorum of the Twelve Apostles. The trip was cut short
when news came that Henry D. Moyle, counselor to President McKay, had died. At the urgent request of President
McKay, the four returned to Utah for the funeral services.

On August 25, 1972, the Haycocks joined President and
Sister Lee and other General Authorities at the area general
conference of the Church in Mexico City. Here the newly
sustained prophet spoke to the Saints in the expansive
National Auditorium in Chapultepec Park, his first visit as

74

head of the Church outside the United States, but his words were for members of the Church everywhere. He said, "The real strength of the Church is to be measured by the individual testimonies to be found in the total membership of The Church of Jesus Christ of Latter-day Saints." He then quoted from the Doctrine and Covenants 88:73: " 'Behold, I will hasten my work in its time.' The evidence of the hastening of which the Lord spoke can be found in no greater measure than in this land of Mexico and in the countries of Central America as witnessed by the overwhelming super-abundance of the blood of Israel to be found here."

At an official dinner for Mexican officials and Church leaders, one of the perceptive local dignitaries engaged President Lee in a discussion. He had been watching the prophet as he spoke individually to members, calling them by name, stopping to encourage here or to quietly counsel there. The diplomat knew he was speaking with a church leader who knew his flock. He asked, "What are you going to do, President Lee, when the Church gets big? So big, you don't know all the names?"

The Church was big, and getting bigger at a rapid pace. When President Lee was called as an apostle on April 10, 1941, the Church had 892,080 members. When he became president on July 7, 1972, there were 3,218,908. "In my judgment, few, if any leaders in the Church had a better understanding of priesthood and church government, save the Prophet Joseph Smith, than President Lee," says Arthur, who had witnessed changes in every aspect of the Church since the late 1930s. President Lee was the primary author of the area conferences, the system of regional representatives, and the correlation program. "He brought the worldwide Church together in one whole, ready to move ahead with force and energy. That was his major contribution."

Before serving as an apostle, President Lee had established and administered the Church welfare program in the 1930s under the direction of the First Presidency. At the time, the United States was reeling from the effects of the Great Depression. Overwhelmed with the magnitude of the assignment to care for the physical needs of Church members, he went up City Creek Canyon, near downtown Salt Lake City, to be alone with his thoughts. He mused about the possible systems that might be put in place to meet the needs of the members. He was thinking in grand terms when he received unmistakable inspiration. Arthur remembers from their discussions, "The answer was simple. All that was necessary was already established: simply follow the priesthood lines of authority." President Lee repeated that example many times when plans were presented to handle the growth of the Church.

Serving as the leader of the new welfare system was not always easy. At times Elder Lee seemed at odds with other areas where the responsibilities seemed to overlap. Arthur was present at a conversation between Elder Lee, newly called as an apostle, and President J. Reuben Clark, a member of the First Presidency for almost three decades. Elder Lee, recognizing the power that came with his new assignment, said, "They'll listen to me now." President Clark nodded in his familiar style and commented, "Yes, they will listen to you. Clearly, you have the authority now, but you be careful how you use it." Many times President Lee repeated that counsel to others as they were called forward to serve and were overwhelmed with their new responsibilities.

"President Lee was the most complex of any prophet I knew," Arthur claims. "He was very thoughtful, deeply spiritual, and very practical. His years of working summers, going door-to-door as an encyclopedia salesman, and presiding over the Pioneer Stake, a stake rich in testimony but not in material wealth, taught him of the realities of life. There was no question in his mind who the Savior was or who the Prophet Joseph was."

President Lee's testimony of the divinity of the work was defined when he told the Saints in general conference in

October 1972: "I know, with a testimony more powerful than sight, that as the Lord declared, 'The keys of the kingdom of God are committed unto man on the earth [from the Prophet Joseph Smith through his successors down to the present], and from thence shall the gospel roll forth unto the ends of the earth, as the stone which is cut out of the mountain without hands shall roll forth, until it has filled the whole earth.' " (*Conference Report*, October 1972, p. 20.)

President Lee did not do the Lord's work alone. He relied on his counselors and the other General Authorities. Marion G. Romney was a dear friend and associate who was called as second counselor in the First Presidency to President Lee in July 1972. He had been ordained an apostle in 1951. Theirs was a special friendship that began in a store one Saturday afternoon when both were working on meetinghouses and needing supplies. Carpenters of a sort, they were shopping the same aisles and began to share experiences. They arranged to see each other again. Their association developed into a friendship based on a similar philosophy about life and their testimonies of the gospel.

President Romney was a man of great integrity, says Arthur. President Romney had a favorite story from his youth that explained his undeviating commitment. When a youth, Marion Romney lived in the Mormon colonies of Mexico. He used to herd the cows home at night for milking. The McClellans and the Romneys had a common lane between their homes. One evening the cows weren't moving fast enough, so Marion picked up some rocks and hurled them at their backs, hoping to hurry them along. He didn't actually aim at the cows but threw the rocks high, knocking some apples down from the McClellans' tree. He scooped them up and arrived home with the apples rolled up in his shirt.

His mother asked where he got the apples, and he said that they fell off Aunt Mary McClellan's tree. Pursuing the incident, she understood that he had knocked them off the tree deliberately. She insisted he take the apples back imme-diately, which he did. Sister McClellan told him to keep the apples, but he learned a valuable lesson. President Romney always said, "From that day on, I have never taken so much as a pencil, a stamp, or a paper clip from the office if it didn't belong to me."

"Every time he wanted to teach about honesty, he talked about those apples," Arthur recalls.

President Lee appeared healthy and vigorous. He kept a busy schedule, balancing travel with his work in the office. He attended the Hill Cumorah Pageant in Palmyra, New York, in the summer of 1973 and with the cast and mission-aries visited the Sacred Grove. Arthur recalls this solemn and spiritual occasion. President Lee told those gathered, "The witness of the Book of Mormon is not found in the ruins of Central and South America. They may be outward evidence of a people long since disappeared. The real wit-ness is that which is found in the Book of Mormon." Then he added, "I know this is the place where the Father and the Son came . . . and the Lord is still standing close to His lead-ers." (*Church News,* August 4, 1973, p. 3.)

President Lee's messages were varied, but the principles were always the same. At a genealogy seminar at Brigham Young University, he said, "Every one of you can become great ancestors. This is the important thing. The only honor to your name is the honor you bring to it." Weeks later, in dedicating a stake center near downtown Salt Lake City, he spoke of the great sacrifice and accomplishments of the early pioneer leaders, many of whom lived in that area. Then he said, "We can equal them in dedication and keeping the commandments of the Lord."

In 1973, the Haycocks accompanied President and Sister Lee to an area general conference in Munich, Germany. The meetings were scheduled on the grounds of the site of the 1972 Olympics.

Munich is known for its beauty and charm, but Arthur

saw only a little of the city from a taxi window on the way to the hotel and out to the Olympic Gardens. He didn't even tour the grounds, still beautifully groomed from the previous year's athletic contests. "These trips were not for pleasure. We worked, we all worked," says Arthur. "Keeping up with the president was a challenge." Arthur credits the pressure to President Lee's vision of the growth of the gospel and recalls how the prophet used to tell the people, "We have only seen the beginning. It is great and significant that doors are being opened in countries where the gospel has not yet been preached to the many faithful of our Father's children."

Arthur and his wife planned to stop off at Spain or Portugal on the way home while President and Sister Lee went to the Holy Land. But when President Lee heard of the plans, he suggested, rather forcefully, that they not take the side trip.

The next morning, before leaving for Jerusalem, President Lee said he had reconsidered and that if Arthur and Maurine still wanted to visit Spain and Portugal, it would be all right with him. Arthur answered, "No, President Lee. Just to know that you had even the slightest question at the wisdom of such a visit is enough for us. We're going home."

President Lee went to Jerusalem with Elder and Sister Hinckley. In Greece they followed the path of Paul. The president spoke to a small gathering of Saints on Mars Hill in Athens and compared the members today with those during Paul's ministry: "As we come to positions of trust and responsibility centuries later, bearing the same message, teaching the same gospel, worshipping the same God, faced with the same opposition, we must not hesitate nor slacken our zeal to project the word of the Lord." (Ibid., December 16, 1972, p. 5.)

President Lee, accompanied by Arthur, went to New York December 19, 1973, to attend a meeting of the Union Pacific board of directors, of which he was a member. When they returned home, President Lee was visibly tired. Traditionally he delivered candy and flowers to friends and neighbors on Christmas Eve. This year, however, Arthur volunteered to make the visits, and President Lee accepted his offer. The prophet spent Christmas day with his wife, Joan, and his daughter, Helen Goates, and her family. He also visited the graves of his first wife, Fern, and his daughter Maurine.

The following day, Arthur collected the mail from the office and delivered it to President Lee, who, at the suggestion of his doctor, had decided to go to the hospital for his annual physical. At three o'clock that afternoon Arthur took him through a back entrance of LDS Hospital and up to his assigned room on the top floor. Sister Lee stayed with them until many of the tests were completed and then went home. Arthur visited with the president while he ate his dinner. "He seemed to be in good spirits and feeling fine," Arthur says.

But the atmosphere soon changed. Arthur was reading the evening newspaper when President Lee turned toward the wall and dozed off to sleep. About eight o'clock, President Lee sat up, spoke briefly to Arthur, and looked as though he was trying to get out of the bed. Arthur began talking to him, but the president didn't respond. "His face was ashen and covered with perspiration," says Arthur, who helped the prophet lie back down and then stepped outside to the nurse's station, about fifteen feet down the hall. The nurse followed Arthur into the room with a wheelchair. Now that President Lee was awake, she said, she'd take him down for an X-ray. Arthur still felt uneasy about the president's condition, so he went to the door and called to a doctor out in the hall. The doctor took a quick look at President Lee and shouted, "Cardiac arrest." The doctor began CPR while the nurse sounded the alarm. Medical people came from every direction with elaborate equipment and, accord-

80

ing to Arthur, "worked heroically and professionally on President Lee."

Arthur called President Romney, who was at home, and explained the unexpected events. He located President Tanner in Phoenix, Arizona, where he was enjoying the holidays with members of his family. Arthur also called Sister Lee and Helen Goates and told them to come to the hospital immediately.

With all the activity up and down the hall and in and out of the room, it became obvious to Arthur that unless the Lord intervened, the president would not live. He hurriedly called Spencer W. Kimball, president of the Council of the Twelve. "When President Kimball answered, he cordially asked how I was, and I responded that I was not very well, explaining quickly that President Lee was very sick," Arthur recalls. "I said, 'I think you should come at once.'" Not until after Arthur had hung up did he realize that he hadn't told President Kimball where to come.

Arthur was waiting down the hall in another room with Sister Lee, Helen, and Brent Goates, President Lee's son-in-law, when President Romney arrived. President Kimball came a few minutes later. Arthur learned a great lesson in priesthood and Church government on that solemn occasion. He explains the events that followed: "President Kimball, president of the Quorum of Twelve Apostles, immediately turned to President Romney, a member of the First Presidency, and asked, 'President Romney, what would you like me to do?' President Romney replied, 'I guess all we can do is pray and wait.' At 9:01 P.M. the doctor came down the hall, shook his head, and said, 'The Lord has spoken. We've done all we can. President Lee is gone.'

"At that precise moment, President Romney, knowing that with President Lee's death the First Presidency in which he had served was now dissolved, turned to President Kimball, who would now become president of The Church of Jesus Christ of Latter-day Saints, and said, 'President Kim-

81

ball, what would you like me to do?' " President Kimball asked President Romney and Arthur to go with him to the Church offices and call the Brethren of the Twelve in various parts of the world to advise them of President Lee's death. A meeting was set to arrange the funeral and to reorganize the First Presidency.

"Just so quietly, so smoothly, the leadership of the Church changed hands," explains Arthur, who had seen this process four times now. "There was no campaigning, no electioneering, no jockeying for position, no speeches—just a simple process the Lord himself has directed, that upon the death of the president of the Church, the president of the Twelve should become the next prophet and president. That is the order of the Church, and the Lord will always have his chosen servant in line when the time comes. That man will have been prepared, trained, tested, and tried. He will be mellowed and endowed from on high, and he will become the president of the Church in the Lord's own way and in the Lord's own time.

"Many considered that President Lee's tenure as president was cut short," says Arthur, "because he had seemed in such good health. He was young and vibrant. But this is the Lord's Church, and he knows what he's doing and when."

Speaking at President Lee's funeral, his dear friend and Church associate President Romney reiterated how President Lee had understood so well his responsibility as prophet: "The source of his greatness was his knowledge that he lived in the shadow of the Almighty." (Ibid., January 5, 1974, p. 12.)

CHAPTER SEVEN

Spencer W. Kimball

For weeks Arthur had quietly accompanied President
Spencer W. Kimball to the Salt Lake Temple. The prophet
was wrestling with a problem that had absorbed much of
his attention. "I remember his wife, Camilla, calling me one
day to ask if everything was all right," says Arthur. "She
asked if something was going on, if there was some serious
problem that had her husband so distressed and concerned."
    Arthur told Sister Kimball that he knew what was trou-
bling her husband, but that he was not at liberty to explain.
"President Kimball was indeed pleading with the Lord for
guidance and inspiration on a matter of major importance,"
he says. He promised Sister Kimball that all was well, and
she thanked him for the reassurance. Only a few days later,
on June 9, 1978, President Kimball, his counselors, and the
Council of the Twelve announced to the world the revelation
that all worthy male members of the Church could receive
the priesthood. President Kimball dictated the declaration to
Arthur, who took it down in shorthand and transcribed it. It
read, in part: "All worthy male members of the Church may
be ordained to the priesthood without regard for race or
color. . . . We declare with soberness that the Lord has now
made known his will for the blessing of all his children
throughout the earth who will hearken to the voice of his
authorized servants, and prepare themselves to receive
every blessing of the gospel."

83

President Harold B. Lee once called Elder Kimball "the biggest short man" he had ever known. President Kimball was a quiet, unpretentious, humble man and a prodigious worker, says Arthur. "He plowed through business all day at the office and then went home for a short nap and a light supper followed by more work and then more work. It wasn't unusual for him to slip down to the office at night if he had something on his mind."

He regularly admonished the Saints to keep a journal, sing in their ward choirs, hold family home evening, plant gardens, pray that doors might be opened in countries not yet admitting missionaries, serve missions, read the scriptures, serve their neighbors, live righteously as families, and repent, repent, repent.

Missionary work and the building of new temples received special attention from President Kimball. When he became president on December 30, 1973, at age seventy-eight, the Church had fifteen temples. In the twelve years he was president, he announced plans for thirty-two more temples, three times as many temples in twelve years as in all the previous years the Church had been organized.

When he spoke to the media at a press conference on September 14, 1974, at the time of the dedication of the Washington Temple, he affirmed that one sign of the growth of the Church was the expansion of temple work. "We teach the truth," he said. "If people knew what we know, there would be great numbers eager to join the Church. It's true, it's right, it's divine."

At a regional representatives seminar less than a year after he had received the mantle of Church leadership, President Kimball spoke in broad terms of the need to expand missionary work, saying, "How can we be satisfied with 100,000 converts out of 4 billion in the world who need the gospel? I wonder if we are doing all we can. . . .We have been proselyting now 144 years. Are we prepared to lengthen our stride?" (*Church News,* November 10, 1985, p. 10.)

The phrase "lengthen our stride" became President Kimball's call to action. "So much depends upon our willingness to make up our minds, collectively and individually, that present levels of performance are not acceptable either to ourselves or to the Lord. In saying that, I am not calling for flashy, temporal differences in our performance levels but a quiet resolve to do a better job—to lengthen our stride."

President Kimball crisscrossed the globe many times as he carried his message to the Saints. A chronicle of the places he visited reads like a geography text: England, Scotland, Poland, the Federal Republic of Germany and the German Democratic Republic, Sweden, Finland, Denmark, Austria, Switzerland, France, the Netherlands, Italy, Greece, Egypt, Israel, the Philippines, Hong Kong, Taiwan, Japan, Korea, Hawaii, American Samoa, Western Samoa, New Zealand, Fiji, Tonga, Australia, Tahiti, Canada, Mexico, Guatemala, Costa Rica, Panama, Peru, Brazil, Argentina, Chile, Bolivia, Colombia, Ecuador, the Dominican Republic, Puerto Rico, Paraguay, Uruguay, Venezuela, and South Africa. He visited some countries many times. In addition, he traveled throughout the United States.

"Everywhere we went, he spread his spirit of warmth and goodness and genuineness," Arthur remembers. Frequently he would remind the people that the Church as a body of mortals can be no more holy than its people are righteous, and he would challenge them to develop Christlike lives of self-mastery. President Kimball loved people, young and old, rich and poor, in high position or no position. All were his friends. He met with presidents of countries, ambassadors, premiers, and prime ministers. He stayed in hotels frequented by world leaders, yet he was always humble in projecting that wonderful, sweet, and articulate spirit of one completely dedicated to the Lord and his children."

President Kimball focused his messages on essential gospel principles. He reminded people to live the commandments. At the first area conference in South America in March 1975, he said: "Father considered long and well the creation of this earth and the peopling of it. . . . He made the earth for our benefit and for our growth and development. . . . You probably do not remember all the things you did in the life before you came here, but you lived; you understood the program; you accepted the divine plan; you agreed to it; you made the covenant, and you must not ignore that promise, even though you have that right of agency." (Ibid., March 8, 1975, p. 4.)

President Kimball understood that all individuals struggle with challenges. His own life had not been easy. His counsel, "Suffering can make saints of people as they learn patience, long-suffering, and self-mastery," had been learned by experience. Over the years he had suffered from various physical problems, including typhoid, smallpox, throat cancer, heart attacks, and open-heart surgery. Once as he was being wheeled to an operating room, the hospital orderly pushing the gurney bumped the corner of the door and began to swear, taking the Lord's name in vain. President Kimball looked up at him and said quietly, "Don't say that. You are speaking about my best friend."

On another occasion, President Kimball was so sick in the South Pacific that he couldn't lift his head from the pillow on the bed. Arthur and Russell M. Nelson, President Kimball's physician who was later called as a member of the Council of the Twelve, dressed the prophet and practically carried him to a waiting police car, which raced them to the airport to catch a flight to another island. He had a temperature of 104, yet he kept going. He would go to a meeting, stand up, and counsel the Saints with great sincerity. Then he would be whisked back to the hotel and put straight to bed to rest before the next meeting.

"He loved the Lord, and he loved the Church; serving them was his life," says Arthur. President Kimball reiterated that love and devotion to a BYU audience on September 6, 1977, when he said: "The Church of Jesus Christ, nicknamed Mormon, is the only true and living church which is fully recognized by God. . . . Most of the world disbelieves it, ministers attempt to disprove it, intellectuals think to rationalize it out of existence, but when all the people of the world are dead, and the ministers and priests are ashes, and the high trained are mouldering in their graves, the truth will go forward, the Church will continue triumphant and the gospel will still be true." (Ibid., September 10, 1977, p. 3.)

Arthur recalls that President Kimball's talks were more than words of inspiration; they were also poetry. "He didn't have a lot of education or a list of degrees behind his name, but he could touch the hearts of people everywhere with his stories and his warm and loving manner."

Arthur's favorite talk was one President Kimball first gave to a congregation in Richfield, Utah, and repeated to other gatherings, including general conference. In it, he talked about "hidden wedges" that could be removed by the process of repentance. "Let those take care who postpone the clearing of bad habits and of constructively doing what they ought. I had learned to use wedges when I was a lad in Arizona, it being my duty to supply wood for many fires in the big house." He then told of a boy who, using a wedge to make his chopping easier, had placed the wedge up in the fork of a tree, planning to take it to the shed right after dinner. He forgot about it.

Years later, as the tree matured, it grew up over the wedge, concealing it completely. During a particularly violent storm, a heavy gust of wind ripped off a big limb, which fell on the roof of the house. When he examined the damage to the tree and the house, the man found the wedge hidden in the fork where he had placed it years before. The tree had grown around it, but the wedge had so weakened the branch that it had fallen because of its unseen weakness. "Pride, envy, selfishness, dishonesty, intemperance, doubt, secret passions—almost numberless in variety and degree—are the wedges of sin. And almost numberless are the men and women who today are allowing sin to grow in the heart wood of their lives.

"The wedge is there. We put it there ourselves one day. It is harming the tree. For years after the wedge had grown over, the tree flourished and gave no sign of its inner weakness. Thus it is with sin. The wedge is there, and in the end of its work is a fallen tree, split, shattered and worthless."

When President Kimball spoke at conferences, he would often outline where he had been, what temple dedications he had attended, the things he had done. He loved people and he loved nature. When he and Arthur used to drive through communities on the way to conferences and meetings, he would say with dismay, "Look at that old barn. Look at that rickety fence. There's a garden that needs tending." At almost every conference, he would counsel, "Paint up, clean up, fix up your homes and your gardens, plant flowers." When he gave a talk at conference entitled "Don't Kill the Little Birds," in which he spoke out against the unnecessary killing of the Lord's creatures, a whole flood of hunting licenses and apologies poured into the Church offices from members who had taken his counsel.

Most happy when he was with the people, President Kimball cared little for visibility or position but a great deal about the needs, wants, and trials of the Saints. His message for finding happiness was uncomplicated: keep the commandments of the Lord. In a conference address in 1974, he said, "We believe that we have in the Church the answers to all the questions, for the Lord is the head of the Church and He has given us the program. Our message is what it has always been, and our hope is that our people will live the

President Spencer W. Kimball and D. Arthur Haycock
at a Church ranch near Orlando, Florida

commandments of the Lord. They have been revealed in the holy scriptures and by living prophets throughout many years."

He was gentle in his manner yet firm and impatient to get things done. He would quietly come out to Arthur's desk and ask, "I wonder if one of the secretaries would have time to type this. I'm in no rush, just whenever they can get to it." Then a few minutes later he would return and ask if his material was ready. He was driven to push the work forward. On his desk was a sign prominently reminding him and his visitors of his motto: "DO IT."

He believed in doing the Lord's work, no matter what. Speaking to missionaries in Mexico, he emphasized the importance of doing more than just being ready to serve: "With missionary work . . . we . . . say, 'Father, Thy will be done.' I'm just Your faithful servant. I'm ready to serve and sacrifice. Open the gates. I'll do it.' The Lord didn't tell Lehi to ask for the plates or to *try* to get the plates. He said, 'Send your sons and *get* the plates.' " (Ibid., December 21, 1974, p. 5.)

When President Kimball succeeded President Lee on

December 30, 1973, there were 3.3 million members of the Church in 630 stakes and 108 missions. When he died in November 1985, Church membership was 5.85 million; the number of stakes had doubled to 1,570, and the number of wards had surpassed 10,000. The number of missionaries serving increased from 18,109 in 1974 to more than 30,000 in 1985. Those figures were a reflection of work—his work. He set the standard, and the people followed. Arthur states firmly, "When I served with President Kimball, I never worked so hard in my life."

The growth of the Church thrilled President Kimball. He said in the opening session of April conference in 1980, "We want to keep faith with that small but noble band of souls who assembled in the Peter Whitmer home 150 years ago for the purpose of formally organizing the Church. We *can* keep the faith, in part, by helping the Church to grow in numbers and also in spirituality." (*Conference Report,* April 1980, p. 6.)

In August 1974, Arthur accompanied the Kimballs to Stockholm, Sweden, for an area general conference for the Scandinavian countries of Norway, Denmark, Sweden, and Finland. Upon arriving, Arthur spent almost all day retyping one of President Kimball's talks on a Swedish typewriter. To the listening Saints, President Kimball suggested that they hang a picture of an LDS temple in their homes to remind them of the work and to increase their commitment to the gospel.

Speaking of the need for local Saints to become involved in missionary work, he said, "Thousands of converts should come in from this source. They are your neighbors. They are your friends. They know your righteousness. You are an example in Christian living to them." (*Church News,* August 24, 1974, p. 4.)

The trip included a tour of Finland with the mission president, Robert Wade, a former member of Arthur's staff in the Missionary Department. In typical Kimball fashion, the tour was packed with events, from dedicating a building to meetings with the missionaries, the Saints, and even the American ambassador to Finland, who commended the missionary force with this comment: "There are only two groups of people who learn the Finnish language, Finnish babies and Mormon missionaries."

This tour brought to focus the rapid growth of the Church in countries all over the world. In 1955 when Elder Spencer W. Kimball visited Europe for six months, stopping at every mission on the continent and in England, his message was clear: "The days of gathering are over, and now we've got to establish Zion in all areas of the world. We need you here. Stay in your homeland and build up The Church of Jesus Christ of Latter-day Saints."

Twenty years later he was back, visiting the members who had taken his admonition seriously and stayed home to build the kingdom. After the tour of Finland, he went to London, where he spoke to some four hundred missionaries and later to more than five thousand members assembled in a stake center.

In February and March, 1975, the Haycocks joined the Kimballs for a tour of South America, beginning with an area conference in Sao Paulo, Brazil. Extra security precautions were taken to prevent any threats or violence to the president and other General Authorities. At a meeting with stake and mission leaders before the conference sessions, President Kimball made the initial announcement of the Church's plans to build the first temple in South America at Sao Paulo, Brazil. He believed strongly in taking the temples to the people and often quoted Brigham Young's statement, "Every time a new temple is built, all the bells in hell begin to ring because Satan knows what it means."

The people in South America were ready for a temple. Arthur recalls the contributions and the sacrifices of so many to bring the temple blessings to their land. One faithful leader gave a gold medal he had received as an army officer after being stranded in the Andes mountains during a violent snowstorm that nearly wiped out his entire troop. The wind was so fierce they couldn't make a fire or put up a tent. To keep their blood flowing, this man and others like him kept moving among the men to help where he could. After twelve days they were rescued, but restoring the use of his frozen hands and feet took years. The country awarded him and the thirty other survivors gold medals for their heroism and leadership. When it came time to make his donation to the Santiago Chile Temple, Brother Cifuentes gave his prized award to be auctioned off to raise funds, knowing that because of the temple great blessings would come to his people. "These people understood that a contribution to the temple was really no sacrifice," Arthur says.

With each new temple came a new set of challenges. Arthur recalls, "When we tried to build a temple in Denver, we had to move the location two or three times because of some public resistance; some people worried that the increase in traffic would create problems. In Chicago, community leaders rejected our original plans because the temple spires would interfere with the flight path of birds migrating for the winter. But in East Germany, the government ran power and sewer lines out to our site and built roads for easy access. When we had the open house at the Freiberg Germany Temple, local leaders from all over East Germany attended. They appreciated that we were admonishing our people to be good citizens. Though our local leaders weren't trained in public policy and diplomacy, they were loyal to their country."

The South American trip also included visits to Santiago, Chile; Buenos Aires, Argentina; Bogota, Colombia; Montevideo, Uruguay; and Asuncion, Paraguay. That swing through South America took the president twenty-five thousand miles. He visited eight countries, toured three missions, and met with the president of Brazil, the prime minister of Paraguay, and the minister of the navy in Buenos Aires.

Everywhere President Kimball went, arrangements were made so he could avoid being crushed by the crowd. Everything was arranged down to the last minute, and President Kimball's departures were carefully planned to get him through the throngs and out of crowded halls. Congregations would stand in reverence, arms folded, as he walked past. But then his love would get the best of him, and he'd reach out and start shaking hands, and everything would break loose. The throngs would swarm around him, and all plans for an orderly exit would vanish.

"That was just his way," says Arthur. "He wasn't kissing babies to get votes or shaking hands to be popular; he was touching the people because he wanted them to know of his love, and he wanted to bless them." Arthur would have to remind himself that the scenarios were something like the one that occurred when the apostles of old turned the children away, and the Lord said, "Suffer the little children to come unto me, for of such is the kingdom of God." (Mark 10:14.)

An incident in Bogota, Colombia, is one Arthur will never forget. The members met in a gymnasium with bleachers from floor to ceiling. A big stage, like a boxing arena, was constructed in the center of the floor as a stand for the General Authorities and local leaders. "These were people who loved President Kimball and were thrilled to be with him," says Arthur. It was planned that ushers would slip President Kimball out the side door just as the closing prayer was announced. However, as the time for departure grew near, President Kimball turned to Arthur and said, "I want to shake hands with the Saints."

Arthur was alarmed. With the final "amen," President Kimball got up, walked out to the edge of the platform, and reached out to shake hands. The members poured off the bleachers like a flood, and those in front were being crushed against the platform by the press of people from behind. Arthur motioned to the security officer in charge, and the

*Attended by D. Arthur Haycock, President Spencer W. Kimball
greets a crowd of well-wishers*

two of them steered President and Sister Kimball safely to the door.

A similar situation occurred in Sao Paulo. Coming out of a big theater where a meeting had been held, President Kimball and Arthur struggled through the crowd to get to their bus, which was waiting out on the street. Arthur was holding on to President Kimball with his left arm and pushing forward with his right when out of the corner of his eye he saw a child knocked to the ground. Arthur instinctively reached down, caught her by the wrist, and pulled her with them fifty feet to the bus. "She'd have been trampled to death by the rush of folks whose eyes were on the departing prophet and not at their feet," he explains.

Arthur would always suggest to the president that he leave the stage early and get to the waiting vehicle before the people descended on them—and President Kimball would always answer the same way: "Now, that wouldn't be fair, would it?"

For many years Arthur observed as the General Authorities reached out to the Saints. "Their love is just a part of them," he says. "They live the gospel rather than just preach it. When you work for those who have time for people, you work for the Lord's chosen." He adds, "It's the people—the ordinary people everywhere, not just the leaders—who make the Church great."

In San Juan, Puerto Rico, the Saints met with the prophet in a large hotel ballroom. Everyone was asked to stand back while the prophet walked out. But their enthusiasm got the best of them, and they crowded forward. Suddenly a woman stood up on a bench, reached out, and whipped President Kimball's head around to plant a kiss on his cheek. Arthur heard his neck crack, and the prophet suffered a stiff neck for days after the incident.

In the Dominican Republic, where meetings were scheduled in a Santo Domingo hotel. President and Sister Kimball were in bed after the last session when Joseph B. Wirthlin, then an Assistant to the Twelve, knocked on the door of Arthur's room with a problem. A group had just arrived from the other side of the island. The crowded bus had broken down from the load, and they had missed the meetings.

Elder Wirthlin had suggested holding a special session for these people at daybreak, but that was impossible. The members had to be back at their jobs in the morning. Arthur went to President Kimball's room to ask permission to express the prophet's love to the people and to explain that the late hour made it impossible for him to meet with them personally.

President Kimball's response was predictable. He looked at Arthur and said, "Now, that wouldn't be fair, would it?" Within five minutes he was dressed and downstairs to meet with this group of dedicated Saints.

All around the world, President Kimball admonished the Saints to live righteously. Typical of his counsel was a message he gave in 1975: "When we are asked by the Lord to enlarge the borders of the Church, that means not only more stakes, more missions and greater missionary work, but greater effectiveness . . . by having more and more of our members, young and old, more fully converted and in control of their lives, and less tossed by the trends of the time." (Ibid., July 5, 1975, p. 3.)

A member of the Twelve Apostles usually accompanied him on long journeys. Elder L. Tom Perry joined him in his visit to the Philippines. When the group stepped off their air-conditioned plane, they were hurried into a waiting air-conditioned taxi and then taken to an air-conditioned hotel. At the hotel, Arthur got out of the car, and immediately his glasses fogged up from the humidity and heat. He took them off and could barely see to get across the lobby and to the elevator. The group included two security officers. When the elevator doors closed, Arthur turned to the tall man behind him and began to clean his glasses on the man's tie. Suddenly he realized that this tie did not look like one either security man had been wearing. He looked up and saw Elder L. Tom Perry looking down—at him. Elder Perry still shields his tie when they meet; undaunted, Arthur always comments, "I'll bet that would be good for cleaning my glasses."

In the Philippines, local authorities assigned two heavy-set men to look after the president. After the meetings, they each took President Kimball by the elbows and walked briskly out of the hall; President Kimball's feet never touched the ground. They had just got him to the car and into the back seat when a missionary approached Arthur and said, "I have to talk with President Kimball." Arthur responded, "You and ten thousand others." The young elder explained, "My companion is new; he's homesick and he wants to go home. He would be a good elder, but he needs some help. I know President Kimball could help him." Arthur, touched by this young missionary who was trying to save his companion, opened the door and explained the situation to President Kimball. "Let me talk to him," said President Kimball. There were hundreds of people jammed in the street and around the car. The missionary's homesick companion entered the car and sat down next to the prophet. President Kimball listened intently to his story. "He didn't scold or lecture," Arthur says. "He just talked to the young elder as if he were his grandfather. Then he patted the missionary on the knee, hugged him, and said a little prayer for him. As the young man climbed out of the car, he said to President Kimball, 'I'm going to stay.' President Kimball knew when to leave the ninety-nine to save the one."

While Arthur was present for many memorable occasions, some of the most wonderful times were an hour here, a half hour there when President Kimball ministered one on one. "There is great security in spirituality," President Kimball said in 1974, "and we cannot have spirituality without service." He called on widows, gave blessings, visited those who were sick. "He did the ordinary things that we so often discount in importance, and yet he understood that in the eternal plan, these were essential," says Arthur. "He did, indeed, live by the exhortation, 'Inasmuch as ye have done it unto one of the least of these, . . . ye have done it unto me.' " (Matthew 25:40.)

In Korea, members attending an area conference in August 1975 arrived in the middle of a heat wave. "I was hotter than I had ever been in my life," Arthur recalls, "but the local people sat very still in the conference. No one even waved a piece of paper or fan for relief." All during the meeting, ushers walked up and down the aisles holding up signs written in Korean. At the conclusion of the sessions, Arthur asked a local leader about the signs and was told that they read, "Please don't use your fans." The people felt that it would be disrespectful to fan themselves in the prophet's presence.

On trips Arthur always carried plenty of cash in the native currency. Still, he never seemed to have enough pesos, pounds, marks, or dollars to keep President Kimball supplied. When the president would meet a boy at a meeting or other function, he'd shake his hand and say, "You're going to be a great missionary when you grow up! This is to start your missionary fund."

"Of course," says Arthur, "they never spent the money. It was a keepsake from the Lord's chosen servant. Some even sent the bills to the office and asked for President Kimball's signature."

President Kimball was particularly vulnerable to requests from children. When he attended a conference in the Southern States one year, it was arranged for him to stay in the home of one of the Saints. Two little boys in the family slept in bunk beds, and they wanted the president of the Church to sleep in their room so they could say, "President Kimball slept here." He and Arthur slept on the small, lumpy beds with squeaky springs. Wanting not to disturb the president, Arthur lay awake on the top bunk most of the night. President Kimball, on the lower bunk, lay awake most of the night trying not to wake Arthur. In the meantime, the boys were sound asleep in a tent on the back lawn.

In February 1977, President Kimball and Arthur were in Mexico City, where they stayed at an elegant hotel overlooking Chapultepec Park and Mexico City. "We'd been to see the president of Mexico and the celebrated cathedral and the Zocalo Plaza," Arthur recalls. "We had seen the rich and famous, the ancient and magnificent sites. Now President Kimball wanted to attend a local family home evening." F. Burton Howard, a stake president from Utah who accompanied them as a Spanish interpreter and representative of the Church's legal affairs in Mexico, was asked to arrange it.

Shortly after dinner, President Kimball and his companions joined the family of Brother and Sister Agrico Lozano, who were of Indian descent. Their humble home was on a narrow street, with their sixteen-year-old car parked outside. The children, dressed in their Sunday best, had prepared a welcome for their guests in their best broken English. The mother gave a talk on the woman of Samaria, and President Kimball played "I Am a Child of God" and "I Need Thee Every Hour" on their piano. At the close of the evening, they all joined in singing "We Thank Thee, O God, for a Prophet." The family presented President Kimball with a book signed by the parents and each of the children. "Imagine the prophet coming to your home for family home evening!" says Arthur. "Yet to him, it was just a chance to be with the Saints."

While in Mexico, the president also made a surprise stop at a Church school. The children were out on the playground, and Arthur encouraged a group of them to run and find their teachers. He chuckles about the reception the children must have received when they announced to their teachers, "The prophet is out in the school yard!"

One brave little boy approached President Kimball and asked where he was from. The response was, "I am from Salt Lake City."

"Oh," said the child, "I thought you were from heaven."

One of Arthur's most memorable journeys with President Kimball was a 1979 trip to the Holy Land to dedicate the Orson Hyde Memorial Gardens on the Mount of Olives. Other Church officials also attended the dedication, including President N. Eldon Tanner, Elder Ezra Taft Benson, Elder Howard W. Hunter, and Elder LeGrand Richards. They visited Nazareth, Bethlehem, Shepherd's Hill, Mount Tabor, the Jordan River, and the Sea of Galilee. They walked on the Mount of Olives and into Bethany, saw the tomb where Lazarus was raised from the dead, and visited the place where David slew Goliath. Indeed, they walked where Jesus walked.

In Jerusalem, a Brigham Young University photographer took photos of President Kimball for a Church film project. The script called for pictures of him walking in the Garden of Gethsemane. A Catholic church had been built there, and the garden was surrounded by a wall. To go into the fenced-off area, it was necessary to obtain permission from the Catholic priest.

The Jewish guide and Arthur talked to the priest, who said that the charge would be 5,000 Israeli pounds per person per minute. For just the photographer and President and Sister Kimball, the fee would have totaled thousands of Israeli pounds, or approximately $450. The guide responded, "No, Father, President Kimball is a holy man. He came here to worship, not to pay tribute." Still, the pictures had to be taken outside the wall.

At the garden tomb, which Joseph of Arimathea had donated for the Savior's burial, the Kimballs and Haycocks stepped though the small opening into the crypt, which had been hollowed out of solid rock. The four of them sat in silence on a bench inside. After some moments, President Kimball began reading aloud from the Bible. He then offered a prayer. "At the conclusion of the prayer," Arthur recalls, "President Kimball turned to the three of us and said, 'I really think this is where they laid our Lord.' "

Everywhere President Kimball went in the Holy Land, Arthur was close to his side. As they walked near the garden tomb where Mary met the Savior that first Easter morning, Arthur held President Kimball's arm. Trailing along behind them was the BYU photographer, who wanted only President and Sister Kimball in the pictures. "I was reluctant to let go of President Kimball because the path was rough and uneven, so I cautioned him to watch his step and be careful," Arthur says. President Kimball turned, smiled, and replied, "It's all right, Arthur. Don't worry. I'm used to walking on holy ground."

A typical day with President Kimball at Church headquarters began early. Arthur always tried to get to work first, but President Kimball also liked to get there first. If Arthur was planning to arrive at 7:30, President Kimball would be there by 7:00. That meant Arthur had to start arriving by

6:30 to have the lights on, the office open, and everything ready when President Kimball came. All his appointments and meetings were outlined.

Arthur always cautioned Church employees to be sensitive and gracious on the phone. He often used as his example an incident that occurred when President Kimball and President Marion G. Romney were attending a meeting in Richfield, Utah. Arthur was taking notes when the stake executive secretary came up to him at the front of the room and said there was an important phone call for President Kimball.

Not wanting to disturb the meeting or the president, Arthur stepped down from the stand and went to take the call. "This is President Jimmy Carter," the caller said. "I would like to speak to your president."

Arthur quickly explained that President Kimball was at the pulpit speaking to a congregation of several hundred people and added, "I know he would like to speak with you, Mr. President. His second counselor is here. Would you speak to him?" Arthur hurried back to the chapel to get President Romney from the stand. President Carter was interested in learning more about the Church's missionary program. He explained that he was going to Mississippi to speak to a convention of Baptists, and he wanted to talk about creating a more effective missionary program—like that of the Mormons. His first question was how many missionaries were serving. President Romney said there were about thirty thousand. Then he wanted to know how much the Church paid them. He was stunned at the response: "Nothing. They all pay their own expenses." President Carter continued with his queries, asking how many countries they served in, where they came from, how they were trained, and how long they served.

Several days later, a newspaper reported on President Carter's speech, quoting him as saying, "We ought to be more like the Mormon Church. They have thousands of young people out teaching the gospel of Christ."

President Kimball thought in terms of "we." When he didn't mean the Church membership in general, he had in mind what would be good for both him and Arthur. They rarely stopped for lunch. The pattern was a result of President Kimball's zeal for the work and an intermittent decision to diet. "He never went on a diet alone," says Arthur. "We always went on a diet together, and he made sure I understood I needed it." The two were the same height, and when President Kimball started talking about Arthur's waistline, it meant they were in for a diet. Some days, hungry, Arthur would suggest lunch, at least a bowl of soup. As he tells it, "I would explain that Sister Kimball would be unhappy if I didn't get him lunch, and the president would quickly retort, 'That's all right. I'd rather she was mad at you than mad at me.' "

In 1975 Arthur accompanied President Kimball on a sentimental journey to his home in Arizona. They stopped in Pima, Thatcher, and Safford to see the homes where the Kimballs had lived, the winding staircase to the attic where Spencer Kimball had read the Bible as a boy, and the Gila Academy where he had been student-body president and a star athlete. They visited the home that Spencer and Camilla Kimball had built and lived in for just three years before Brother Kimball was called to Salt Lake City in 1943 as a member of the Twelve

Spending so much time together, the two men became close friends. They shared sorrows and celebrations; they laughed and they cried. And, like most proud grandfathers, they talked about their grandchildren. Arthur, in particular, liked to share his stories, and President Kimball had heard them all. Returning to the airport from a conference in the South, President Kimball seemed to be dozing in the front seat, so the stake president, who had been driving for more than thirty minutes without a saying a word, asked Arthur if he had any grandchildren. Before Arthur could answer, President Kimball lifted his head and said, "For heaven's sake, don't ask Arthur about his grandchildren. He'll never stop talking, and we'll miss the plane!"

President Kimball had a look of innocence and love that attracted people to him. But, says Arthur, "He also was human; he got frustrated and upset at times, like all the rest of us." He was independent and would sometimes slip out the back stairs when Arthur wasn't looking. Arthur saw his job as always taking care of the president. When they took a ship across the Mediterranean to Israel, President Kimball would deliberately get up and stroll around the ship alone, earlier than the two had agreed, just so he could greet the Saints who were hoping to see him. "I was trying to take care of him," says Arthur, "and he was interested in taking care of everyone else."

When they traveled, they always had adjoining rooms. If their wives were with them, President Kimball always asked Maurine, "You aren't going to lock this door, are you?" Arthur always kept a robe where he could reach it quickly.

When they were walking down the street, Arthur was quick to remind President Kimball of a letter or an accomplishment of someone heading their way. No matter where they were, Arthur always had a paper and pen handy to make a note of a name or an address and phone number. "There was never time for us to relax," he claims. But that didn't bother President Kimball.

President Kimball always advocated righteous living. He understood that the commandments knew no geographical boundaries. In Poland in 1977, when he dedicated the land for the preaching of the gospel, his supplication to the Lord included these words: "Bless these fathers and mothers in this nation, that they may bring up their children in righteousness, that they may train aright and bless the children that they may grow up to be honorable, peaceful, loving parents themselves, so that the generations may

bring to Thee, their Lord, great satisfaction in the development of the souls of men." (Ibid., September 1977, p. 3.)

The General Authorities are serious about their work,
but most of them also have a good sense of humor. "I still
remember an amusing experience on the plane when I
returned from Canada with President Kimball and several of
the members of the Twelve," Arthur says. A flight attendant
asked one of the Brethren if he would like some coffee. He
said that he would like some lemonade. She responded that
she didn't have any lemonade. She was moving off down
the aisle when she must have remembered that she had
some lemons. She came back and said, "I can squeeze you
some." He replied, with a twinkle in his eye, "Don't touch
me."

People flocked around President Kimball and sometimes
tried to take advantage of him. When he was in the hospital,
one of those attending him asked for the inside scoop on the
Second Coming. His response was quick: "Why? Are you
ready to go?"

"He got scores of requests to perform marriages and
attend special functions," according to Arthur. "One man
tried to get a commitment from me that the prophet would
perform his marriage in the temple. Since President Kimball didn't know him, I turned him down. He apparently
wouldn't take no for an answer, because a short time later he
stood in front of the prophet's house and caught him coming home from work." The next day President Kimball
scolded Arthur for being too protective. He had agreed to
perform the wedding Arthur had declined for him

President Kimball's love for the Saints took him to Idaho
after the collapse of the Teton Dam in 1976. A twenty-foot
wall of water had wiped out many businesses, homes, and
farms and forced residents of this fertile farm country to flee
for their lives and then return to start over. At the time of the
disaster, President Kimball had been flying home from a
conference. The plane had developed engine trouble, and

*President Spencer W.
Kimball and his wife,
Camilla Eyring Kimball,
harvesting oranges at a
Church orchard in Florida*

the president's party was stranded in Colorado. He didn't
hear of the dam's collapse for more than twelve hours after
it occurred. Arthur says, "He was visibly shaken that he had
not been able to respond more quickly. The next day we flew
to Idaho and toured the area by helicopter. Meeting with the
Saints in temporary quarters, he encouraged reconstruction,
telling them, 'Rebuild your lives while rebuilding your
homes.' "

With all his humility, President Kimball also had a feisty
streak. He would say that he got that trait from his grandfather Edwin Woolley, explaining, "If my grandfather ever
drowned in a swift-running river, you wouldn't look for him
downstream. He was so contrary, he would float upstream
after he drowned." Arthur says, "When President Kimball
got something on his mind, he would not let go of it. He
was tenacious and determined yet demonstrative and kind."

President and Sister Kimball were always frugal. Sister
Kimball had learned to make ends meet while growing up

in the Mexican colonies, where food and clothing were scarce and making do was a way of life. She always tended a garden and bottled fruit and vegetables. When they moved into the Hotel Utah, she still went home to their residence to pick the apples from their tree in the backyard. She would cart them down to the hotel, up the elevator to the top floor, and down the hall to their apartment so that she could make applesauce. She bottled tomatoes, pears, beans—whatever she had in sufficient quantity. Arthur remembers stepping onto the elevator in the lobby of the Hotel Utah and smelling chili sauce. It was Sister Kimball's spicy home-cooked recipe simmering on the stove up on the tenth floor.

For President Kimball's eighty-fifth birthday party, she prepared a tribute that she shared with all attending: "On this your eighty-fifth birthday, my beloved husband, my heart is full of gratitude for the sixty-two years we've been privileged to share. They've been filled with joy and sadness. Sharing has made the joy more fulfilling and the sadness easier to bear. You have been patient with my foibles and richly fulfilled my needs. Your love and understanding have helped me over the rough spots. Our travels around the world have brought joyful and rewarding memories. In addition to my great love for you, I deeply respect and honor your undaunted courage in meeting successfully the many challenges which have filled your life. Your complete and unwavering dedication to your callings and service to others has been a lifetime of inspiration to me."

When President Kimball traveled, he took no time out for sightseeing. He claimed to have seen all of the world he wanted to see and was singularly focused on laboring for the Lord. On a European tour in 1977, he and Arthur had a week's break before going to Warsaw, Poland, to finalize arrangements for official recognition of the Church in that land. Arthur thought it a fine time to visit England, the land of his father's birth. President Kimball had different ideas. He wanted to visit the four new missions in Italy, as well as those in Austria and Germany. They went to Italy. Their first morning there, President Kimball asked when the meetings were scheduled with the missionaries. Wanting to conserve the president's strength, Arthur had planned a free day with an evening session. "I'm just trying to save you, President," Arthur said. Spencer Kimball responded, "I know you're trying to save me, but I don't want to be saved. I just want to be exalted."

Arthur set up meetings with the missionaries in every city they planned to visit, including Milan, Rome, Sicily, London, and Berlin. President Kimball's attitude was always the same: "You can't just float down the Thames; you have to be up and going. You've done a great job so far. Now what are you going to do tomorrow? Quicken your pace, lengthen your stride."

When President Kimball attended a meeting or a conference and got tired, he would ask to use the bishop's office for a few minutes; then he would shut the door and lie down on the floor for a quick nap. Soon after he became president of the Church, Arthur found him sleeping on his desk and promptly went out and bought a couch for the office.

"President Kimball was driven to do the Lord's work, and it showed," says Arthur. His shoes frequently needed resoling because, as he often said to Arthur, "My life is like my shoes, to be worn out in the service of the Lord." When he sat on the stand with his legs comfortably crossed, those in the audience could see the soles of his shoes worn right through.

In May 1980 more than 75,000 Latter-day Saints gathered at the Pasadena Rose Bowl in Southern California for an area conference. President Kimball was seated on a platform under the east goalposts, and during the meetings, he occasionally crossed his legs for comfort. A few days later a letter came to him at the Church offices with a check for forty dollars inside. A man who had viewed the proceedings through binoculars had observed that President Kimball had a hole in the sole of his shoe. In his letter he asked that the money be used to purchase a new pair of shoes for the prophet.

Arthur put the forty dollars into the general missionary fund and then went straight to a Salt Lake clothier and selected three new pairs of shoes, each a different style, in the president's size. President Kimball chose the pair he liked best and put them on. Arthur threw away the well-worn shoes.

The next day the two men left for a two-week trip to South America. Every day of the journey, President Kimball complained that his new shoes were too stiff, pinched his toes, rubbed his heels, and were uncomfortable. He rued the day Arthur convinced him to trade his perfectly good, though well-worn, shoes for a new pair.

Arthur tried to tailor his schedule to match President Kimball's. Planning to attend an event at the Lion House one evening, President Kimball stayed in his office working and waiting for Sister Kimball. About 5:30 he urged Arthur to go home, but his secretary insisted on staying as long as he did, saying, "President, you're making this hard for me. I am torn between doing my duty to stay close to you and still doing what you ask me to do." President Kimball, with a twinkle in his eye, responded, "They both ought to be the same, hadn't they?"

President Kimball took the process of perfection seriously. When in Kirtland, Ohio, he met a distant cousin who was not a member of the Church, he treated him the same way he treated everyone else, with thoughtfulness, interest, and great regard. The cousin, quite taken by President Kimball's sincerity and kindness, suggested to Arthur, "They should make my cousin Spencer a saint." A Catholic, the cousin was paying President Kimball a high compliment. When Arthur mentioned the cousin's praise to President Kimball, his response was immediate: "Nobody can make me a saint. I have to do that for myself."

President Kimball's philosophy was always to put the Lord first, others second, and himself last. Even when he was ill and unable to work in the office, nothing was on hold. "He had set the agenda, and we simply followed his directions," says Arthur.

That President Kimball began to suffer physically from age and illness in the last years of his presidency was not unusual. "It's a reality of life," says Arthur, who has been at the bedside of five presidents of the Church when they died. "The president, quite naturally, is an older man when he is ordained and set apart, having already served many years as a member of the Council of the Twelve. Usually he has been in that position as a special witness of Christ for more than thirty years."

Arthur recognized the signs of wear on President Kimball as they were preparing to come home from a meeting at Logan, Utah, in the spring of 1979. President Kimball was leaning to one side, and Arthur, who was supporting him, worried that he might have had a stroke. He called President Kimball's physician from Logan and arranged to meet him at his clinic in Salt Lake City so he could check the president. When they had trouble getting President Kimball out of the car, they went immediately to the hospital.

That evening, after all the tests and CAT scans, a neurosurgeon recommended operating at once. President Kimball was suffering from a subdural hematoma.

"I determined I could not go through this alone and tried to get President N. Eldon Tanner on the phone," says Arthur. After repeatedly getting a busy signal on the Tanner number, he called Elder G. Homer Durham, a member of the Council of Seventy, who lived in the same building and on the same floor as the Tanners, and asked him to alert President Tanner. It seemed like only minutes had passed when President Tanner walked through the door. That night President Tanner and Arthur each slept on a hospital bed while they waited for word about the success of the surgery. At 3:00

A.M. the doctor woke them to explain that President Kimball had come safely through the operation and was out of danger.

Arthur often looks back on how Gordon B. Hinckley was called into the First Presidency just when the prophet and the Church needed him most. President Kimball hadn't been well, but one day he suddenly appeared stronger. He came out to Arthur's desk on July 23, 1981, and said he had decided to call another counselor. "See if you can find Elder Gordon Hinckley for me," he said to Arthur.

"Before I do that, President," said Arthur, "I want to be the first to hold up both hands to sustain him. We have worked closely together for more than forty years, and he is my dear friend."

President Kimball next asked Arthur to find Elder Neal A. Maxwell, one of the presidents of the Seventy, who was in the hospital following surgery. President Kimball and Arthur went immediately to the hospital, and President Kimball called Elder Maxwell to be an apostle, to fill the vacancy created by President Hinckley's becoming a member of the First Presidency.

"There was no doubt about it," says Arthur, "President Kimball needed some additional help in the presidency." President Tanner was gravely ill, and President Romney was not well. President Hinckley was well prepared to give faithful and able assistance. "President Hinckley was always careful not to push himself forward or assume prerogatives that belonged to the prophet," says Arthur. "He understood he had been called to help, and he did just that in any way he could."

President Hinckley had been a Church employee since 1935, three years longer than Arthur. "The Lord prepared President Hinckley for these days," says Arthur. "Over the years he'd had a depth of experience with the media, with temple work, as a member of the missionary committee, and with Church finances. He'd served on several boards of directors. With his wealth of experience, he was a great strength to President Kimball and an important addition to Church leadership."

Arthur describes President Kimball as a true servant of the Lord, always about his Father's business. "You can imagine his frustration when due to age and failing health he was unable to lengthen his stride or even maintain his pace in pushing forward the work of the Lord," says Arthur.

President Kimball's health began to fail shortly after President Hinckley's call, and he never again regained his strength. President Tanner passed away four months later, and President Romney's health continued to decline. The last time Arthur saw President Romney was shortly before his death. His eyes were closed, and he could barely move. Arthur sat down at his side and said, "President Romney, it's Arthur. If you can hear me, squeeze my hand." President Romney did.

In April 1982 President Kimball stood at the Tabernacle podium and delivered a brief testimony. It was a prophetic farewell when he said, "As I express that love for you and for the memory of the great experiences I've had with you, I bear my testimony: This work is divine, the Lord is at the helm, the Church is true and all is well." It was the last conference address he would present at general conference. His next conference sermon was read by Arthur, his secretary.

In 1980 Arthur spoke to an audience of students about his years with President Kimball, telling them: "We've been a lot of places together. We have laughed and sung the hymns together. We've prayed together. We've walked and ridden horses together. We've slept in the same room. I sat with him at breakfast this morning. He's old. He's tired. He's worn out. Unless the Lord heals him, he'll never go traveling again. But he is the prophet, and he will live as long as the Lord wants him to be president of the Church. I encourage you when you sing, 'We thank thee, O God, for a prophet to guide us in these latter days' that you sing with feeling and meaning and determination to follow his counsel. It won't always be what you want or what's convenient or what you enjoy, but I can testify to you, if you do follow him, always, you will never stray on forbidden paths. Your lives will be happy, and you will hear a glorious welcome when you pass to the other side, 'Well done, thou good and faithful servant. Enter into the joy of the Lord.' "

President Kimball's physical condition continued to weaken. Still he wanted to meet with people. He attended general conference, but it was exhausting for him. "I remember helping him when he attended all four sessions a month before he died," says Arthur. President Kimball died November 5, 1985. He was ninety years old.

CHAPTER EIGHT

Ezra Taft Benson

On May 1, 1992, the day before the Bountiful Temple site was to be dedicated, Arthur, as he had done so many times before at similar sites around the world, was walking around the area, "just making sure everything was in order."

This time, however, he wasn't on official business. He had retired from full-time Church employment by now and was serving in the Salt Lake Temple as a sealer.

Arthur no doubt understood better than most what this new temple would do for the community, the Church, and the work for the dead. He was sensitive not only to the grand affair scheduled for the next day but also to the long-range impact of this new temple in Zion. The location was well chosen, on a hillside overlooking the Great Salt Lake. It would be easily accessible from the Davis County suburbs, just north of Salt Lake City, much as the Jordan River Temple was accessible to Saints in the south part of the Salt Lake Valley.

Arthur wasn't alone. As he walked around the rough ground, President Ezra Taft Benson arrived to make a similar survey. For both it was a joyous meeting, and they shared their exhilaration for the event that would come the next day.

"I asked him how he was doing," Arthur says, "and in his typical style, he beamed and drew me to him. 'I love you,' he said. There we were at the site of another temple to be constructed for the Lord. It was a setting like so many others we had shared in our lives. But you never get used to a prophet of the Lord saying, 'I love you.' We both shed tears as we embraced."

President Benson and Arthur shared much in their five decades of association. Called as a General Authority in 1943, President Benson began his service to the Church with President Heber J. Grant. Arthur worked with him then and during President George Albert Smith's tenure. In 1952, when Elder Benson took on the additional responsibility of running the U.S. Department of Agriculture and serving in the Eisenhower Cabinet, Arthur was asked to assist in the new assignment. On leave of absence from the Council of the Twelve, Elder Benson left for a fact-finding tour around the United States while Arthur began organizing the myriad requests and information that began pouring into Secretary Benson's office. He also began poring over publications describing agricultural issues around the country.

In January 1953, Arthur and Daken Broadhead, a member of the Church who was originally from Nephi, Utah, accompanied the new Secretary of Agriculture to Washington, D.C. Both would serve as his assistants. Life in Washington was a sharp contrast to the religious environment of Salt Lake City. The tenor of activity at the Department of Agriculture was intense. On Secretary Benson's desk was a special white phone linked directly to the White House. "When Secretary Benson used it, you knew something official and important was coming," Arthur says.

Secretary Benson, in his honest and trusting style, expected complete integrity and veracity from others in Washington. But such was not always the case. Many times Arthur went home disappointed in the way Secretary Benson had been misunderstood and misrepresented. "Here was a man totally dedicated to doing what was right and necessary operating amid many who had agendas of their own," says Arthur.

*Secretary Benson
and his assistant,
D. Arthur Haycock*

A Washington reporter observed in 1954 that Secretary Benson "acts like a man whose conscience is always clear— his testimony will be the same next week or the week after or a year from now." Speaking not of his spiritual witness but of his truthfulness before Senate committees, the reporter said, "He doesn't have to remember what he said to an opposition senator at the last meeting. This is a built-in ulcer-saving device, not always found in Washington."

The Washington experience had another side, however. The Haycocks joined the Secretary for a gala affair at the White House with President Eisenhower and his advisors and were included in other major events. "Secretary Benson welcomed us and treated us kindly in every circumstance," says Arthur.

In the fall of 1953 Arthur accompanied Secretary Benson to a convention of agricultural leaders at the Waldorf Astoria Hotel in New York City. Secretary Benson's address focused on issues and trends facing agriculture across the country. Near the close of his remarks, he paid tribute to a successful agribusiness leader from Chicago, lauding the man's contribution not only to the agriculture industry but to the country as well.

A few days later, Secretary Benson received a letter from the man expressing appreciation for the compliments and honor. It was what Arthur calls a "bread-and-butter" thank-you to a high government official; the letter said all the right things in just the right way. But what impressed him most was the postscript penned at the bottom of the letter in a firm executive hand. It read, "Secretary Benson, since I was with you in New York I have had the strangest feeling that I wanted to leave my nets and come follow you and be a fisher of men."

"President Benson so radiated his spiritual strength and closeness to the Lord that though his talk was about agriculture, a far greater message reached this man's heart," Arthur says. "A prominent Catholic, this man had seen beyond Secretary Benson's political role to his spirit. He knew, indeed, that he had been with a man of God."

While Elder Benson served eight years in Washington, Arthur was called, after a year and a half, to return to Church service as mission president in Hawaii.

Arthur later worked again with President Benson, serving as his secretary in the first months of his presidency of the Church. "He came into the office with sincerity and purpose," Arthur says. He focused quickly on the three-fold mission of the Church—to proclaim the gospel, to perfect the Saints, and to redeem the dead. "We shall continue every effort to carry out this mission," said President Benson.

"President Benson is thoughtful of others," Arthur comments. "When I was asked to return to Hawaii to work in the temple in 1986, he personally, without being asked, made arrangements for Maurine and me to take my ailing ninety-five-year-old mother with us on the assignment. I was visiting her daily and caring for her, and he knew she could

116

President Ezra Taft Benson and his wife, Flora Smith Amussen Benson

not be left alone in Salt Lake City." Arthur's mother did not make the journey to Laie; she died shortly before their departure. Arthur relates, "I was touched that President Benson, President Monson, and other Church authorities took time from their busy lives to attend her funeral. President Benson asked to speak as well."

"President Benson is a man of wisdom, loyalty, character, and dedication," Arthur says. "His great loves are country, family, church, and the Book of Mormon. No one has ever put more emphasis on the divinity of the Book of Mormon and the importance of its message in our lives.

"I love him dearly, not only as the leader of the Church but also as my friend. We have shared much of our lives together; we have seen much change in the Church."

As he looks back over his life, D. Arthur Haycock claims to be just an ordinary man who has had extraordinary experiences. His life's mission has indeed been unique. He has learned how to get up early, work hard, and do all he can to contribute to the building of the kingdom. "For more than fifty years, I worked closely with, listened to, and observed the unselfish service and wise counsel and example of truly great men," says Arthur. "My experiences have been rewarding beyond earthly expectations. You can't work at the side of such chosen vessels of righteousness without recognizing that the Lord is in charge and that his servants are his witnesses. I have traveled the world with them, worshiped with them, prayed with them, and joined in sacred priesthood ordinances. With each I have found an understanding heart. My experiences far outweigh any material blessings or missed opportunities. I am so fortunate, so blessed, to have spent my working years in the company of prophets."

Index

119